Navigating Love: Dating Odyssey in Century

A comprehensive guide for modern women: from online dating to conflict management, discovering authenticity, and growing through every experience

Simon Love

1.

Introduction:

- The Importance of Self-Awareness in the Dating World.

- What Does "Playing the Game" Really Mean in Dating?

2. History of Dating:

- How Dating Dynamics Have Changed Over Time.

3. Self-Awareness and Self-Evaluation:

- The Importance of Knowing Oneself Before Entering the Dating World.

4. Defining Your Values:

- What Do You Truly Want from a Relationship?

5. The Importance of Communication:

- How to Communicate Your Needs, Desires, and Boundaries.

6. Expectations vs. Reality:

- The Difference Between What We See in Movies and What Happens in Reality.

7. Online Dating:

- Navigating the World of Online Dating, Pros and Cons.

8. Safety First:

- Tips and Tricks to Ensure Your Safety During Dates.

9. Chemistry and Compatibility:

- How to Recognize the Difference and the Importance of Both.

10. Handling Rejection:

- How to Confront and Overcome Rejection in the Dating World.

11. The Art of Flirting:

- Techniques and Tips for Flirting with Authenticity.

Introduction

In the vibrant and ever-evolving world of dating, one thing has remained constant: the need for self-understanding and awareness. While the dating landscape has transformed with the advent of new technologies and cultural shifts, the importance of deep self-awareness before diving into this adventure cannot be underestimated.

Self-Awareness: This is not just a simple cliché or a self-help manual phrase. It is a profound and ongoing process of reflecting on one's needs, desires, values, and expectations. In a world where we are often encouraged to compare ourselves to external standards – be it romantic movies, Instagram stories, or well-intentioned friends' advice – it is essential to come back to ourselves. Only with a clear understanding of what we want and who we are can we enter the dating game with a defined direction and authentic vulnerability.

And here we come to the concept of "playing the game" in dating. What does it truly mean? Many people see it as a set of strategies to "win" someone's attention or affection. Others view it as a role-playing game, where we are actors in a drama we hope will have a happy ending. But "playing the game" can be something much deeper and more meaningful. It can be about expressing one's authenticity, establishing genuine connections with others, and learning along the way. It's not about manipulation or wearing a mask, but about showing up authentically, with our strengths and flaws, and finding someone who appreciates us for who we truly are.

In light of this, this book will explore how to navigate the dating world with integrity, authenticity, and a solid understanding of oneself. We will offer tools, advice, and reflections to help every woman find her way, regardless of external expectations. Because, in the end, the true "game" of dating is not about conquest but connection.

Welcome to this journey of self-discovery in the world of dating. And now, let's begin.

In the modern era of dating, where swiping left and right dominates our search for a partner, self-awareness emerges as the anchor that can keep our boat steady amidst these tumultuous waters. Dating apps, while extraordinary tools for expanding our potential partner pool, can also lead to a certain depersonalization of the dating experience. In this context, a clear understanding of what we want and who we are becomes even more crucial.

Think of self-awareness as an inner compass. In a sea of profiles, messages, and first impressions, it can be easy to get lost in the noise or feel overwhelmed by expectations – both our own and those of others. But with a solid compass, we can navigate with determination, avoiding being pulled in directions that don't reflect our true desires or values.

However, self-awareness is not something acquired overnight. It requires introspection, reflection, and sometimes even the courage to face uncomfortable truths about ourselves. It might mean admitting that we fear commitment or acknowledging that in the past, we allowed the wrong people into our lives due to low self-esteem. It might also mean understanding that what we want from a relationship now may be different from what we wanted five or ten years ago.

As we embark on this journey of self-discovery, another concept emerges strongly: "playing the game." The term "game" often carries negative connotations when it comes to dating, suggesting manipulation tactics or a dishonest approach. But if we view it from a different perspective, "playing the game" can represent the path of learning and adaptation we go through in the world of dating.

In fact, every interaction, every date, and every relationship (regardless of its duration) offers us a lesson. These lessons, if observed and assimilated, sharpen our ability to understand ourselves and what we want from a partner. They teach us to recognize the behaviors we appreciate and those we won't tolerate. They show us how we might react in certain situations and how we might want to react in the future. And, ultimately, they help us play better, in the sense of having more authentic, honest, and rewarding interactions.

Moreover, "playing the game" can also reflect our ability to remain open and curious. Even if we've had bad experiences in the past, every new person we meet is a unique individual with their own stories and lessons to offer. Approaching the dating world with an attitude of curiosity rather than cynicism allows us to see each new interaction as an opportunity rather than a potential minefield.

This doesn't mean we should ignore red flags or blindly dive into situations that feel wrong for us. It simply means that armed with our inner compass of self-awareness, we can approach the dating world with a balance of caution and openness, ready to learn, grow, and ultimately find a connection that truly resonates with who we are.

2. Dating History: How Dating Dynamics Have Changed Over Time

Reflecting on the history of dating provides us with a lens through which we can observe not only the evolution of romantic relationships but also the socio-cultural, economic, and technological changes that have influenced this evolution. The art and dynamics of courtship have undergone multiple metamorphoses, each leaving an indelible mark on how we perceive and approach love today.

Antiquity: In ancient civilizations such as Greek and Roman, dating and marriage were often transactions designed to secure political or economic alliances between families. Romantic love, as we conceive it today, was not necessarily the foundation of these unions. However, this does not mean that love and passion did not exist; they simply had a different role in the overall social structure.

Medieval Period: During the medieval period, the concept of chivalrous courtship emerged in Europe. Knights and ladies courted each other through poetry, songs, and romantic gestures, often idealizing the object of their affection. Yet, despite the notion of romantic love, many unions were still arranged based on economic or social considerations.

Victorian Era: With the Victorian era came rigid norms and rituals surrounding courtship. The "calling" became a common practice, where a young man would visit a young woman at her home, always under the supervision of an adult. Discretion and propriety were paramount.

1920s and 1930s: The early 20th century saw a greater liberalization of dating. The automobile, for instance, played a crucial role, allowing couples more privacy and autonomy. The concept of "going out" informally became more popular, especially among young people.

1960s and 1970s: The sexual revolution of this period led to a drastic revision of traditional norms regarding dating and relationships. Free love and women's liberation profoundly changed the dynamics and expectations surrounding dating.

1980s and 1990s: With the advent of early chatrooms and phone dating services, technology began to play a role in the dating world, albeit in a very different way from today.

2000s and Beyond: The digitization of dating has taken center stage. Websites like Match.com and later apps like Tinder revolutionized how people meet and interact. The speed and convenience of these platforms gave individuals greater choice, but also brought new challenges such as choice overload and superficiality.

Today, as we find ourselves in an era where personal autonomy and freedom of choice are at the forefront of the dating scene, it is crucial to remember how past dynamics have influenced and shaped the present. The history of dating shows us that while methods and expectations may change, the pursuit of connection, understanding, and love remains a constant of the human experience.

Following the explosion of digital dating platforms in the early 2000s, there has been a continuous evolution of dating dynamics. The influence of social media, for example, has made online "presentation" almost as important as face-to-face interactions. Facebook, Instagram, and other platforms have offered people the opportunity to build and curate a public image, thus influencing first impressions and perceptions in budding relationships.

In parallel with the rise of social media, the speed and efficiency of modern dating apps have also given rise to the phenomenon of "ghosting" (the act of disappearing without explanation from a relationship or conversation). This is fueled by the seemingly endless array of options available and the relative ease of avoiding difficult conversations in a digital environment.

Another significant change has been the increase in globalization in the dating world. With apps and websites connecting people from different parts of the world, long-distance relationships, once considered an exception, have become much more common. This globalization has also led to greater cultural exchange, with individuals navigating the challenges and beauties of intercultural relationships like never before.

Simultaneously, with the advancement of technology and digitalization, there has also been a return to the roots in some aspects of dating. "Slow dating," for instance, is a movement that encourages people to take their time in getting to know potential partners, emphasizing the quality of interactions over quantity. This can be seen as a reaction to the frenzy and choice overload offered by traditional dating apps.

Additionally, as dating apps have become the norm, there has been a growing awareness of safety challenges associated with meeting strangers online. This has led to innovations such as integrated video chats, stricter safety controls, and other features designed to make online dating a safer experience.

Gender fluidity and the broadening understanding of sexual identities have also left an indelible mark on the modern dating landscape. Apps like Grindr, HER, and other platforms specific to the LGBTQ+ community have offered new opportunities for connections that were once marginalized or ostracized. Acceptance and understanding of diverse identities and sexual orientations have led to a more inclusive and diverse dating landscape.

Lastly, the recent COVID-19 pandemic has had a significant impact on the dating scene. Lockdowns and social restrictions have limited face-to-face interactions, pushing people further towards digital platforms. Virtual dates, video calls, and online interactions have become the norm, forcing individuals to find new ways to establish authentic connections through screens. This period has also led many people to reflect on their priorities in terms of relationships, with many recognizing the value of deep and meaningful connections over superficial bonds.

In the context of the post-pandemic dating scene, new trends and challenges have emerged. One of these is the growing importance of "pandemic compatibility." This refers to individuals seeking partners who share their views and practices regarding health safety, vaccination, and pandemic-related behaviors. This new dimension of compatibility has added an additional layer of complexity to the already intricate world of dating.

In parallel, forced physical distance has reignited an interest in traditional forms of communication. Many have rediscovered the charm of handwritten love letters, thoughtfully chosen gifts, and well-planned virtual dates, often mimicking real experiences such as watching a movie together or having a candlelit dinner via video call. This "old-school" courtship has offered a nostalgic break from the frenetic digital nature of modern dating.

Dating dynamics have also been influenced by the growing global discussions on topics like social justice, gender equity, and climate change. "Values compatibility" has become increasingly relevant, with many individuals seeking partners who not only share personal interests but also have aligned views and commitment on global issues. Dating apps like OkCupid have started including questions related to social and political themes, allowing users to see where they stand on these crucial issues.

Furthermore, there has been a growing recognition of the need for mental well-being in the dating scene. Awareness of the mental and emotional challenges associated with dating, such as dating anxiety, social pressure to find a partner, or managing past relationships, has led to a greater emphasis on emotional support and the importance of communication. Many are seeking relationships where mental health and self-awareness are valued and prioritized.

In the context of technology, augmented and virtual reality has also begun to make its appearance in the dating domain. Though still in its infancy, the idea of having virtual dates in three-dimensional environments or using augmented reality to enhance physical dates presents endless possibilities for the future. Imagine being able to explore a digital city together or having an augmented reality "filter" during a date that provides information or fun activities.

Finally, there has been a growing desire for authenticity. In an era of curated profiles, influencers, and often-filtered reality, many people are seeking authentic and genuine connections. This has led to an appreciation for imperfections, personal stories, and real-life experiences. In a world saturated with superficial connections, depth and sincerity have become rare and precious commodities. As the dating scene continues to adapt and evolve, the pursuit of a true and meaningful connection remains, as always, at the core of the human desire.

The history of dating, as we have traced, deeply reflects the evolution of society and its priorities. Starting from ancient times when dating and unions were often instrumental for political or economic purposes, to today, in a digital era where the possibilities for connection are nearly infinite, we have witnessed profound changes in the dynamics of love and courtship. But with this evolution have also come new dilemmas.

The introduction of technology has certainly expanded the horizon of romantic opportunities, but it has also introduced unprecedented challenges. In a world where a match or connection is just a click away, the question arises: what does it truly mean to connect with someone? This question has led many people to seek authenticity amidst a seemingly infinite array of options.

Recent global crises, such as the COVID-19 pandemic, have further complicated the dating scene, introducing new dimensions of compatibility and emphasizing the importance of communication and empathy. They have also underscored the fragility and value of human connections, prompting many individuals to deeply reflect on what they seek in a partner.

The current dating landscape, with its combination of advanced technology and a growing desire for depth and authenticity, represents a crossroads. People now navigate a delicate balance between appreciating the new opportunities offered by technology and the intrinsic desire for deep, authentic, and meaningful connections.

History has shown us that, despite challenges and changes, the pursuit of love and connection is a constant of the human experience. And just as past generations found ways to navigate the dynamics of their time, the modern individual adapts, learns, and grows in this ongoing evolution of the game of love. Ultimately, the history of dating is a reflection of our unending aspiration to understand, connect, and, in the end, love and be loved in a continually changing world.

3. Self-Awareness and Self-Evaluation: The Importance of Knowing Oneself Before Entering the Dating World

Self-awareness is the key to understanding and recognizing one's own feelings, motivations, desires, and fears. It is the foundation from which we can understand what drives us, what holds us back, and how we interact with others. When it comes to dating and relationships, self-awareness becomes even more crucial. Here's why.

Understanding Your Values and Desires: Before seeking a partner or entering a relationship, it's essential to have a clear understanding of what values mean to us and what we want from life. This allows us to find a partner who shares or respects these same values and aspirations, creating a solid foundation for a long-term relationship.

Recognizing Behavioral Patterns: We all have behavioral patterns that manifest in relationships, often rooted in our past experiences. Being aware of these patterns helps us avoid falling into repetitive behavioral traps that can harm our relationships.

Managing Expectations and Boundaries: The ability to set and communicate our boundaries, as well as to understand and manage our expectations in a relationship, is essential. Entering the dating world with a clear understanding of what you can tolerate and what you desire allows for healthier relationships and avoids disappointments.

Improving Communication: Self-awareness influences the ability to communicate effectively. When you know your emotions and reactions, it becomes easier to express them constructively and actively listen to your partner.

Preventing Self-Loss: One of the dangers of relationships is the possibility of "losing oneself" in the partner, especially if you lack a clear understanding of who you are as an individual. Self-awareness serves as a compass, guiding us to maintain our individuality even within a relationship.

Promoting Personal Growth: Lastly, the ability to self-evaluate and recognize areas for personal growth is fundamental not only for our personal development but also for growth within a relationship. A deep understanding of oneself enables proactive handling of challenges, both as an individual and as a partner.

In summary, entering the dating world with a solid self-understanding provides a stronger foundation on which to build relationships. This self-awareness not only enhances the quality of relationships but also our own happiness and satisfaction within them. While the dating scene may change and evolve, the need for self-awareness and self-evaluation remains a constant, fundamental aspect of finding and maintaining meaningful and lasting relationships.

While self-awareness serves as a fundamental pillar in the quest for authentic and lasting relationships, the act of self-evaluation serves as a complement, consistently guiding our journey of inner growth.

Every interaction, every date, and every relationship presents unique learning opportunities. When we approach dating with a reflective attitude, we can see these moments not only as steps toward finding the right partner but also as mirrors that reflect aspects of ourselves that might otherwise remain hidden. For example, an unexpected emotional reaction during a date might reveal old wounds or insecurities that we haven't yet addressed.

Similarly, understanding and recognizing one's own needs in a relationship can be a challenge. Many enter the dating world with preconceived notions of what they seek in a partner, based on societal norms, family expectations, or past experiences. However, these preconceived ideas can often cloud our ability to see what we truly need. Self-evaluation allows us to distill these needs, separate them from external expectations, and focus on what genuinely brings us happiness and satisfaction.

Furthermore, the ability to self-evaluate leads to greater resilience in dating. The reality is that not every date or relationship will be successful. There will be disappointments, broken hearts, and moments of doubt. However, with a solid self-understanding, these challenges become less discouraging. Instead of viewing these moments as failures, self-evaluation enables us to see them as opportunities for growth and learning.

Likewise, awareness of one's strengths and weaknesses can profoundly influence the dynamics of a relationship. For example, if a person knows they struggle with communication when stressed, they can adopt strategies or have a dialogue with their partner about this aspect, creating an environment of understanding and support.

Confidence is another crucial aspect in the world of dating, and self-awareness is closely tied to building strong self-esteem. When you know your own worth and are aware of your abilities, you are less likely to settle for relationships that don't meet your standards or fall into toxic dynamics.

Finally, considering the increasingly digital nature of modern dating, with its wide range of apps and platforms, having a clear understanding of oneself can help navigate this sea of possibilities with a sense of direction and purpose. Rather than feeling overwhelmed by infinite options, those with strong self-awareness can approach the world of online dating with a clear vision, effectively filtering opportunities that truly reflect what they are looking for in a partner and a relationship.

In the deep journey of self-understanding, a fundamental truth emerges: every individual is a unique combination of experiences, expectations, dreams, and fears. While the world of dating can often seem like a complicated puzzle, the key to navigating it successfully largely lies in our ability to understand and accept ourselves.

Within the context of dating, self-awareness influences not only the type of partner we attract or seek but also how we approach and overcome challenges. For example, jealousy is an emotional reaction that many people experience in a relationship. However, for those who are aware of their insecurities and fears, jealousy can be addressed not as a sign of problems in the relationship but as an opportunity to address and resolve unresolved personal issues.

Similarly, awareness of one's attachment styles can deeply influence how we approach relationships. Are we avoidant, anxious, or secure in our attachment styles? Understanding these tendencies can illuminate not only why we behave a certain way in a relationship but also which types of relationship dynamics may be healthier for us.

In the modern world, where the concept of love and relationships is constantly influenced and shaped by movies, TV series, social media, and popular culture, it's easy to lose sight of what it truly means to have an authentic connection with another individual. Here, self-awareness serves as an anchor. It allows us to separate romanticized expectations from reality and guides us toward relationships based on truth, honesty, and mutual understanding, rather than unrealistic ideals.

Many relationship experts also emphasize the importance of mindfulness or "mindful awareness" in the world of dating. This practice, rooted in meditative traditions, involves the ability to remain present and aware in the moment. For those who practice mindfulness in dating, there is greater capacity to truly listen to a partner, perceive one's emotions without judgment, and act in ways that are in line with one's authentic values and desires.

Furthermore, awareness of one's personal "red flags" or personal warning signs can be a powerful tool in the world of dating. These are often derived from past experiences and represent behaviors or traits that a person knows are not compatible with their long-term happiness or well-being. While it's important to remain open and not too rigid in one's expectations, having clarity on what constitutes a potential warning sign can protect against toxic or unsatisfying relationships.

Lastly, we cannot overlook the power of vulnerability. Being self-aware doesn't just mean recognizing and acting on our strengths, but also accepting and embracing our imperfections. Vulnerability, when shared in a context of trust and respect, can create deep and lasting bonds, as it allows two people to see and accept the full range of human nature, both in its light and shadow.

In the context of dating and relationships, self-awareness and self-evaluation are not mere buzzwords or fleeting ideals. They are instead fundamental tools for effectively navigating the complex fabric of human interactions and building strong, lasting relationships. Through deep introspection, we gain a better understanding of who we are: our strengths, weaknesses, desires, fears, and expectations. This awareness allows us not only to select compatible partners but also to address conflicts and challenges with greater balance and wisdom. Rather than reacting impulsively or being guided by the emotions of the moment, we can respond with intentionality and clarity, always keeping in mind what is in our best interest and that of the relationship.

Recognizing and Understanding Your Behavioral Patterns, Needs, and Attachment Styles can lead to greater clarity in relationships. We are better equipped to establish healthy boundaries, communicate effectively, and avoid traps or toxic dynamics. This clarity not only leads to healthier relationships but also to a greater sense of personal satisfaction and fulfillment.

Furthermore, in an era where technology and social media have transformed and, in some cases, complicated the dating landscape, **self-awareness** stands as a guiding light. It navigates us through the tumultuous waters of online dating, helping us discern between superficial connections and potential partners with whom we can build authentic and lasting bonds.

In conclusion, while the dating world may be ever-evolving, the need for self-awareness and self-evaluation remains constant. These are the tools with which we can construct our personal narrative in the dating world, a narrative that reflects our truth, values, and vision of love and partnership. Entering this world with a solid understanding of oneself not only enhances the quality of our relationships but also allows us to approach the search for love with confidence, courage, and authenticity.

4. Defining Your Values:

- ### What do you truly want from a relationship?

The concept of "values" often evokes ideas of morality or ethics, of what is right or wrong in a universal context. However, when we talk about values in the context of personal relationships, we refer to something much more intimate and personal: the guiding principles that determine what we consider most important and meaningful in our interactions with others.

Defining your values in a relationship is not a theoretical exercise, but rather a journey of introspection and reflection that can illuminate the path to an authentic and fulfilling connection. Here are some key considerations:

1. **Personal Priorities and Aspirations:** Before trying to figure out what we want from a partner, we must understand what we want for ourselves. This may include career goals, personal aspirations, family desires, or even the direction in which we want our spirituality to grow. Clarity in these areas can help us choose partners who respect, share, or at the very least, support these aspirations.
2. **Emotional Needs:** Every individual has fundamental emotional needs: the desire to feel loved, valued, understood, and safe. Identifying which of these needs are most crucial to you helps you communicate them effectively and seek partners who are willing to meet them.
3. **Personal Boundaries:** Boundaries are not only protective barriers but also affirmations of what we consider acceptable or not. These can pertain to issues such as physical intimacy, financial management, relationships with friends or family, or any other aspect of daily coexistence.
4. **Shared Core Values:** While opposites may attract, shared core values are often what keeps a couple together in the long run. This could involve matters of faith, political views, work ethics, or views on parenting.
5. **Defining "Success" in a Relationship:** The success of a relationship is not measured solely in years spent together but in the quality of those years. Do you want a quiet and stable relationship, or one filled with adventures and discoveries? Defining your personal "success"

helps you navigate the waters of relationships with a clear compass.

6. **Growth and Change:** Relationships, like individuals, grow and change over time. Defining your values also means recognizing and honoring your potential for growth and change, and seeking a partner who not only grows with you but encourages your growth as an individual.

Ultimately, when we reflect on the question "What do you truly want from a relationship?" we are trying to understand how we want to feel, how we want to be treated, and what kind of life we want to build with another person. This requires courage, honesty, and, above all, a deep sense of self-awareness. However, it is this inner journey that leads to the deepest, most meaningful, and satisfying relationships. In a world where relationships can often seem complex and overwhelming, having a clear understanding of your values can serve as a compass, guiding you toward connections that truly resonate with your heart and soul.

In the fabric of human relationships, personal values clarity acts as a sort of filter. Every time we interact with potential partners or navigate the context of an existing relationship, these values underscore, often imperceptibly, our decisions, reactions, and expectations. Consider values as a kind of DNA of relationships; they don't dictate every single action, but strongly influence the overall course of things.

After all, we live in an age of limitless choices. With dating apps and globalization, potential connections are just a click away. But with this abundance of options comes a sort of paradox: how do you choose, and on what basis? Here, personal values become essential. It's not just about selecting a partner based on a checklist of requirements but rather having a deep sense of what truly resonates with you.

For instance, for some people, loyalty might be a core value. They might have grown up in families where loyalty was a pillar, or they may have experienced past instances where a lack of loyalty caused deep pain. For these individuals, the ability to completely trust a partner and feel secure in the reciprocity of that trust is essential.

For others, personal growth might be at the center of their value network. They may seek partners who challenge them, introduce them to new ideas or experiences, and are as passionate about learning and development as they are.

Likewise, there are people for whom independence holds particular significance. They admire and seek partners who respect their space and autonomy while also desiring to maintain a degree of independence even within a close relationship.

Even the concept of family varies greatly from person to person. For some, family means having children and building a home together. For others, it might mean traveling the world together or building a community of friends and loved ones. For still others, it could mean having pets or dedicating themselves to causes and communities.

And then there are the little things, which often aren't so small. How do you want to spend your leisure time? What's your approach to money and finances? How do you feel about traditions and celebrations? These aspects, although they may seem trivial at first, are deeply rooted in our personal values and influence our relationships in ways we may not immediately recognize.

But one of the most beautiful aspects of values is that, even though they can be profoundly personal, they can also be incredibly universal. Everyone, regardless of their background, culture, or personal history, needs love, connection, respect, and understanding. And while the way we interpret or experience these needs may vary, the core of these desires remains the same. And when we recognize and honor these values, both in ourselves and in others, we create space for truly deep and transformative relationships.

Defining your values in the realm of dating and relationships is not a static task but rather an evolving journey. This is particularly true in a constantly changing world, where new experiences and challenges may lead us to reconsider or reaffirm what we deem important.

In many cultures, for example, the value of tradition carries significant weight in relationships. Family history, cultural and religious traditions, and community expectations can form a backdrop against which we measure our relationships. For some people, respecting these traditions is crucial, while for others, the freedom to choose a different path is equally vital. This tension between tradition and modernity can influence partner choice, relational dynamics, and even the vision of the future together.

In the modern context of dating, we also have the value of technology. How do digital platforms influence our perception of relationships? For many, the ease of connection offered by dating apps can seem like both a blessing and a curse. On one hand, it provides an opportunity to meet people outside of our immediate social circle. On the other hand, it can also create an illusion of abundance, where the next potential connection is always at your fingertips, making it challenging to focus on and invest in a present relationship.

And what about compatibility? In an era where science and technology offer us DNA-based compatibility tests or matchmaking algorithms, how do we balance trust in science with intuition and personal experience? Compatibility can be based on a range of measurable parameters, but also on the mysterious "click" or "spark" that many people believe lies at the heart of a truly special relationship.

The question of values also extends to our attitudes toward conflict. How do you handle disagreement in a relationship? Do you believe in direct confrontation, or do you prefer a peaceful and harmonious resolution? Your response to these questions is closely linked to your core values regarding respect, communication, and the importance of harmony in a relationship.

Finally, there's the matter of authenticity. In a world where we're often encouraged to present a filtered version of ourselves, both online and offline, how do we remain true to ourselves and our values? Authenticity in a relationship doesn't just mean being genuine with your partner but also with yourself. It means acknowledging your flaws and insecurities, accepting your ambitions and desires, and having the courage to show up authentically, even when it may feel vulnerable.

In this vast landscape of considerations, it's evident that values are not just words written on a piece of paper. They are the compass that guides every decision, every interaction, and every expectation in a relationship. And while challenges and circumstances may change, having a clear understanding of your values provides a solid foundation on which to build authentic and lasting connections.

Defining your values is not merely an act of introspection but represents the construction of a sturdy foundation for all future relationships. In the labyrinth of modern relationships, these values serve as a compass, guiding us through complex choices and moments of uncertainty. They help us recognize not only what we desire in a partner but also what we expect from ourselves within a relationship.

Every value we identify and honor becomes a pillar in the structure of our relationships. For example, if we value authenticity, we commit to living with sincerity, favoring transparency and truth in every interaction. If respect is at the core of our values, it will guide every action, ensuring that every decision, big or small, is made with consideration for the feelings and needs of others.

However, recognizing your values doesn't mean that navigating the world of dating immediately becomes simple. On the contrary, it can present new challenges. You might encounter individuals who don't share or respect your values, or you might find yourself having to reaffirm your values in challenging situations. But having clarity about what constitutes your internal compass provides you with invaluable guidance, a point of reference that allows you to move through the world of dating with confidence and authenticity.

In conclusion, in the context of an ever-evolving world where dating can seem increasingly complex and elusive, returning to the foundations of your values provides essential clarity. This clarity will not only influence your choice of partner but also shape the dynamics and quality of the relationships you build. Through defining and adhering to your values, you create a context in which relationships can flourish in sincerity, respect, and authentic love.

5. The Importance of Communication: How to Communicate Your Needs, Desires, and Boundaries

Communication is the lifeblood of every relationship. Beyond romantic sunset walks or candlelit dinners, it is through communication that two people build mutual understanding, resolve conflicts, and deepen their bond. But communication is not just about speaking; it also involves listening, perception, and the ability to authentically express what one feels inside.

Expressing Your Needs

Needs are fundamental to our well-being. They can pertain to emotional security, the need for love, attention, or autonomy. Communicating your needs is not a sign of weakness but rather an act of self-awareness and courage. Here are some steps to do it effectively:

1. **Self-reflection:** Before communicating your needs to others, you must first understand them yourself. Take a moment to reflect on what makes you feel balanced, loved, and secure.

2. **Be specific:** Instead of saying, "I wish we spent more time together," you could say, "I'd like to have a weekly evening just for the two of us."

3. **Use "I" in communication:** Express your needs in terms of how you feel or what you desire, rather than in terms of what the other person is not doing. For example, "I feel appreciated when you listen attentively" rather than "You never listen."

Expressing Your Desires

Desires concern the things we want but are not essential, unlike needs. Communicating desires can enrich the relationship and bring greater satisfaction to both partners.

1. **Share your dreams:** Talk about your aspirations, the things you want to do or experience together.

2. **Be open to compromise:** While desires are important, it's essential to be flexible and willing to find common ground.

Setting Boundaries

Boundaries are crucial for a healthy relationship. They protect your personal integrity and create a clear distinction between what is acceptable and what is not.

1. **Define clearly:** If you don't want your partner to read your messages without your permission, express it clearly.

2. **Be consistent:** Once boundaries are set, it's essential to maintain them. Consistency helps build trust and mutual respect.

3. **Respect others' boundaries:** Just as you want your boundaries to be respected, ensure you do the same for your partner.

As we delve into the facets of communication in relationships, it becomes evident that communication is not merely the act of conveying information. It is, rather, an intricate weave of language, empathy, active listening, and the ability to negotiate common meanings. In relationships, especially in romantic ones, the stakes are even higher because the quality of communication can directly impact the duration and relational satisfaction.

Body Language

Body language is an essential part of communication, often overlooked. Studies suggest that a significant percentage of our communication is non-verbal. This includes gestures, facial expressions, eye contact, and posture. For instance, while a partner's words may express agreement, their body language, such as avoiding eye contact or crossing their arms, may suggest otherwise. Being attuned to both your partner's and your own body language can significantly enhance mutual understanding.

Empathy and Active Listening

Empathy is the ability to put oneself in another's shoes, to feel what they feel, and understand their perspective. This skill is fundamental in relationships. Paired with active listening, where you pay full attention to the other person without interrupting or forming mental responses, empathy can create a safe environment where both partners feel seen and understood.

Digital Communication and Relationships

In the modern era, digital communication has taken a dominant role in relationships. Text messages, chats, video calls, and social media offer new ways to connect. However, digital communication also presents unique challenges. Without non-verbal cues, it can be easy to misunderstand the tone or meaning of a message. Couples must learn to navigate this digital landscape, ensuring that technology enriches rather than hinders their connection.

Feedback and Constructive Criticism

Every relationship goes through moments where providing feedback or addressing issues is necessary. The key lies in doing so constructively. Using the "sandwich" technique, where criticism is framed between two positive comments, can make communication less confrontational. It's also helpful to avoid accusatory language and generalizations, such as "you always" or "you never."

Conflict Management

Even in the best relationships, conflicts arise. What distinguishes healthy relationships from less healthy ones is how these conflicts are handled. The key is to see conflict as an opportunity to grow together rather than as a battleground. This involves avoiding blame, actively listening, and seeking win-win solutions.

At the heart of communication lies the desire for connection and mutual understanding. Despite the challenges that may arise, both in the early and advanced stages of a relationship, it is through continuous, open, and honest communication that couples can build a solid foundation for lasting love.

Communication, as often observed, is both an art and a science. This multidimensional aspect is particularly evident in interpersonal relationships, where spoken (or unspoken) words can have a profound and lasting impact. But beyond spoken words, there are many other levels of communication that influence romantic interactions.

Emotional Intelligence

At the core of effective communication is emotional intelligence (EI). EI includes the ability to recognize, understand, and manage one's own emotions, as well as to recognize, understand, and influence the emotions of others. In romantic relationships, a strong EI can help navigate communication challenges like misunderstandings, emotional wounds, or differences of opinion. The ability to tune into one's own emotions and those of the partner can significantly reduce conflicts and promote mutual understanding.

Tuning In and Presence

In an era dominated by technology, where distractions are always at hand, being truly present during a conversation has become a rare art. Tuning in involves the ability to be fully present and attentive to your partner, showing genuine interest in what they are saying. This kind of undivided attention not only values what the other person has to say but also strengthens the emotional bond between partners.

Cultural Codes and Communication

People come from different cultural backgrounds, and each culture has its unique set of communication codes. These may pertain to how emotions are expressed, how conflicts are managed, or even how often and openly certain topics are discussed. Recognizing and respecting these cultural codes is crucial, especially in intercultural relationships, to avoid misunderstandings and to enrich the relationship through the sharing and appreciation of differences.

Vulnerability

Being vulnerable means showing authenticity, with all your imperfections, fears, and desires. Vulnerability can be seen as a risk, but it is also a powerful form of communication that can lead to greater intimacy and understanding. Through vulnerability, partners can share their deepest insecurities, hopes, and dreams, creating a space of safety and trust.

Resonance and Reflection

Another fundamental aspect of communication is the ability to reflect what the partner has shared, showing that they have been heard and understood. This can be done through resonance, which is the act of "resonating" with what the other has said, and through reflection, which involves repeating or paraphrasing what has been said for confirmation.

Communication in a relationship goes beyond mere transmission and reception of information. It is an intricate dance of emotions, verbal and non-verbal language, presence, tuning in, and authenticity. While words are powerful, it is often silent gestures, shared glances, and moments of silent understanding that speak louder than any spoken sentence.

In conclusion, communication goes far beyond mere verbal expression. It is an intricate weave of empathy, understanding, listening, and vulnerability. In a relationship, especially a romantic one, the quality of communication often determines the depth and duration of the bond.

For many people, learning effective communication skills is a journey that requires time, awareness, and practice. The first step is to recognize the importance of clear and honest communication, always respecting the other person's perspective and emotions. The key is to seek to understand before being understood. This mutual perspective facilitates the creation of a safe environment where both parties can freely express their feelings, desires, and concerns.

In addition to words, effective communication requires a deep understanding of non-verbal signals, such as body language and tone of voice. These often-overlooked elements can convey messages as powerful, if not more so, than words themselves. Therefore, developing sensitivity to decode and respond to these signals can greatly enrich interactions.

Communication is also influenced by various external factors, such as cultural context and personal experiences. This means that each individual will have their own unique style and set of expectations when it comes to communicating. Recognizing and appreciating these differences is essential to building bridges of understanding and avoiding potential sources of conflict.

In conclusion, communication is the foundational pillar on which all meaningful relationships are built. It requires ongoing commitment, a willingness to learn, and the ability to adapt and grow. Only through effective communication can couples hope to build a lasting and profound connection based on trust, respect, and authentic love.

6. Expectations vs. Reality: The Difference Between What We See in Movies and What Happens in Real Life

The romantic portrayals we see in movies, TV series, and novels have had a significant impact on our perceptions and expectations of love relationships. These media tend to idealize love, presenting it as a journey without obstacles or with obstacles that can be easily overcome with grand gestures of love. But how much of this representation actually reflects in everyday life? And how do these expectations influence our real relationships?

The Presentation of the Perfect Beginning

In movies, love stories often begin with chance encounters that seem to be destined by fate. Whether it's in the rain at a bustling city intersection or accidentally bumping into each other at a coffee shop, these moments are depicted as magical and predestined. In reality, while such encounters can indeed happen, many relationships begin in a much more ordinary way, through mutual friends, at work, or in online environments.

Grand Gestures vs. Small Moments

Movies love to showcase grand romantic gestures: running to an airport, serenading under the window, or elaborate marriage proposals. But in everyday life, love is often built through small daily acts, like making coffee for your partner in the morning or listening to their concerns after a long day. These moments, while less theatrical, are fundamental for building an authentic connection.

Conflicts and Resolutions

In media, conflicts between partners tend to be dramatic and intense, often resolved with a revelation or heroic gesture. In reality, conflicts can be more nuanced and require deep communication, understanding, and compromise to resolve. There is no quick or magical solution; instead, strong relationships are built on the ability to work together through difficulties.

Fiction vs. Imperfection

Movies often feature characters with few real flaws, or flaws that are actually charming or easily accepted. In reality, each of us has imperfections, insecurities, and personal challenges. Accepting and loving someone despite, or perhaps because of, these imperfections is what makes love authentic and enduring.

The Duration of Love

While media stories tend to focus on infatuation, passion, and the intensity of new love, they offer fewer representations of the challenges and joys of long-term relationships. The reality of love is that it evolves, changes, and deepens over time, through the challenges and joys of everyday life.

While romantic stories in the media immerse us in worlds of unstoppable passion and eternal love, the reality of relationships often comes with quite different shades. Some of these nuances, not always reflected on the big screen, include:

Personal Growth: Movies rarely show the importance of personal growth in a relationship. In the real world, individual evolution is crucial. Two people may start a relationship from a certain point, but both will change over time. The key is to grow together, learning and adapting to each other, rather than growing apart.

Everyday Life: If movies were an accurate representation of life, we might think that relationships consist solely of candlelit dinners, exotic trips, and passionate discussions in the rain. But real relationships are also made up of daily routines: grocery shopping together, arguing about who should empty the dishwasher, or deciding what to watch on TV on a quiet evening.

Compromises: Movies rarely show the small and large compromises that couples make every day. Whether it's deciding where to live, how to manage finances, or how to spend holidays, real relationships require a constant balance between the needs and desires of both partners.

External Challenges: In addition to internal challenges in a relationship, there are also external challenges like work, health, family, and friends. These factors can create tensions and complications that are rarely explored in depth in the media.

Friends and Family: In movies, the love story is often at the center of the plot, with little room to explore how external relationships influence the couple. In real life, friends and family play a huge role. They can support the relationship or create tensions, and learning to balance these external relationships is crucial.

Mental Health: Few movies address the importance of mental health in a relationship. Issues like depression, anxiety, or bipolar disorder can have a significant impact on a couple. Understanding and addressing these challenges are essential for the health of the relationship.

Technology: In an era of social media, dating apps, and digital communication, technology has transformed how people start and maintain relationships. This new landscape presents both opportunities and challenges, from long-distance relationships made more manageable through technology to tensions created by digital misunderstandings or social media jealousy.

The reality of relationships is that they are complex, multifaceted, and ever-evolving. The nuances of real relationships, with all their imperfections and challenges, are what make them authentically beautiful.

Time and Its Demands: The notion of time, as portrayed in movies, always seems sufficient. Couples in movies appear to have all the time in the world to solve problems, go on adventures, or rekindle lost passion. In reality, time is a precious resource. Finding quality time to nurture the relationship amidst the demands of work, family, and personal commitments can be a challenge.

Relationships are rarely portrayed realistically in films. While in fiction, we often see dominant characters making all the decisions, the reality of modern relationships tends to strive for balance. This balance requires constant effort and communication to ensure that both parties feel heard and valued.

Cultural and Religious Differences: Films tend to standardize and simplify relationships, often overlooking the challenges and beauties that arise from cultural or religious differences. In real relationships, these differences may require understanding, learning, and adaptation.

The Evolution of Desire: Contrary to the perpetual idea that passion is always high in movies, in real life, desire can fluctuate and evolve. There can be periods of distance and periods of renewed intimacy. Confronting and accepting these changes is essential for the longevity of a relationship.

The Impact of Technology on Privacy: The digital age has introduced new challenges to privacy in relationships. The temptation to "spy" on a partner through social media or electronic communication can create distrust and tension. Defining digital boundaries is an essential part of setting expectations in a modern relationship.

Managing Pain and Loss: While movies might show a romanticized view of grief or loss, the reality is much more complex. Whether it's the loss of a job, a family member or friend, or a past trauma, how we deal with pain will profoundly influence our relationships.

The Economics of a Relationship: Films rarely delve deeply into the economic challenges within relationships. From decisions about who pays during a date to managing shared finances to planning for the future, economics plays a crucial role in many relationships.

Health and Well-being: In addition to mental health, physical health can profoundly affect a relationship. Illnesses, long-term health issues, or even divergent fitness habits can create tensions and require adjustments from both parties.

In conclusion, the complexity of real relationships far surpasses that of their cinematic counterparts. While movies often offer a sanitized and simplified version of love, reality provides a rich, deep, and often unpredictable plot that couples navigate together. This intricate dance between two individuals is what makes each relationship unique and, in many ways, even more fascinating than any Hollywood scenario.

In summary, the comparison between expectations fueled by movies and the reality of daily relationships is as fascinating as it is complex. While the media, while being a source of inspiration and entertainment, can sometimes create distorted or idealized expectations. The risk is perceiving the reality of relationships as a failure or disappointment when they do not conform to these cinematic standards.

Authentic relationships are rich in nuances, conflicts, joys, challenges, and moments of growth. They are woven with silences and unspoken words, compromises, and small daily victories. Away from the Hollywood spotlight, in homes and everyday lives, relationships thrive on authenticity, understanding, and a constant commitment to adaptation and mutual growth.

While movies can offer moments of escapism and romance, real relationships require work, patience, and a deep understanding not only of the partner but also of oneself. They require the ability to communicate, set boundaries, face challenges together, and celebrate successes. Where movies often end with a "happily ever after," the reality of relationships is that they are an ever-evolving journey rather than a definitive destination.

Ultimately, while it's crucial to enjoy and draw inspiration from the media, it's equally crucial to have a clear and realistic view of what a relationship means and requires. Only through understanding and accepting the nuances and complexities of real relationships can we aspire to build deep, meaningful, and lasting bonds.

7. Online Dating: Navigating Between Virtuality and Reality

Virtual Navigation: Online dating has radically transformed the landscape of romantic encounters. Thanks to digital platforms, you can "meet" someone without ever leaving your home, browse profiles like you flip through the pages of a book, and chat with people from all over the world. This convenience has made the search for a soulmate accessible to anyone with an internet connection.

Pros of Online Dating:

1. **Wide Selection:** Dating apps and websites offer a vast number of profiles to choose from, increasing the chances of finding someone with similar interests and goals.

2. **Convenience:** You can search, chat, and arrange dates from the comfort of your home, making the quest for love more flexible than traditional methods.

3. **Filtering:** Many platforms allow you to filter profiles based on specific criteria like interests, age, religious beliefs, etc., making the search more targeted.

4. **Preliminary Communication:** Having the ability to chat online before a real-world meeting can help break the ice and establish an initial level of comfort.

5. **Opportunities for Specific Niches:** There are specialized sites and apps for particular niches or interests, such as animal lovers, vegans, or art enthusiasts, making it easier for people with common passions to connect.

Cons of Online Dating:

1. **Dishonesty:** Not everyone is truthful in their profiles. People can lie about their age, appearance, job, and other personal details.

2. **Option Overload:** Sometimes, an abundance of choices can become overwhelming, leading to the so-called "analysis paralysis" or the phenomenon of always thinking the grass is greener on the other side.

3. **Emotional Disconnection:** Communicating through a screen can limit the ability to read non-verbal cues and create a genuine emotional connection.

4. **Safety Risks:** Meeting strangers encountered online can pose risks. It's crucial to take

precautions, like meeting in public places and informing friends or family about the date.

5. **Hidden Costs:** While many dating platforms are free, others require subscriptions or payments for premium features, which can add up over time.

Navigating with Wisdom: Despite the challenges, online dating remains a valuable tool in the modern dating world. The key is to approach the process with an open mind but also with caution. It's essential to remain authentic, be clear about your values and desires, and not be afraid to take breaks if the experience becomes too intense or stressful.

In conclusion, online dating, like any other tool, has its pros and cons. Its effectiveness largely depends on how it's used and the attitude with which it's approached. With the right combination of caution and optimism, it can become an effective means to find that special connection.

Algorithms and Connections: One of the magic behind many online dating sites is the use of algorithms. These complex mathematical calculations assess users' responses to specific questions and attempt to match individuals based on compatibility. However, these algorithms are not infallible. Even if two people might seem compatible on paper, chemistry and real-time connection may not be present. Similarly, you might meet someone with whom you seem to have little in common and discover that the connection is surprisingly strong.

The Paradox Effect: Paradoxically, having too many choices can lead to a feeling of dissatisfaction. This is known as the "paradox of choice." In a sea of profiles, the search for the "perfect person" can become endless. You might go from one profile to another, thinking the next one could be better or more suitable. This continuous search can actually hinder the ability to settle down with someone and build a meaningful relationship.

The Importance of Photos: The first impression is everything in the world of online dating. Photos are often the initial point of contact. However, it's essential to remember that a photo is just a snapshot, a moment captured in time. It doesn't tell the whole story of a person or the depth of their character. Additionally, the widespread use of filters and photo manipulation can distort reality, creating unrealistic expectations.

Ghosting and Other Trends: One of the most frustrating and painful challenges of online dating is the phenomenon of "ghosting," where someone suddenly disappears without explanation. This trend, along with others like "breadcrumbing" (sending sporadic messages without a real commitment) or "zombie-ing" (returning to someone's life after a period of absence), reflects some of the emotional complexities and evasive behaviors that have emerged in the digital age of dating.

Mindset Shift: For many people, the key to successfully navigating the world of online dating is to change their mindset. Instead of seeing it as a way to find the perfect soulmate, it can be helpful to view it as an opportunity to meet new people, experiment, and learn more about oneself. This doesn't mean lowering standards but rather opening the mind to different possibilities and approaches.

Feedback and Reviews: Some platforms offer features where users can leave feedback or reviews about their dates. This can be helpful to gain insight into how you come across on dates and what you might work on. However, it's crucial to take these reviews with a grain of salt and not let them overly affect self-esteem or self-perception.

Social Media and Online Dating: With the advent of social media, the boundary between online dating and social networking has significantly blurred. Platforms like Instagram, Facebook, and Twitter have unofficially become new meeting grounds. This has led to the emergence of spontaneous relationships born from comments, direct messages, and shares.

However, this has also introduced new dynamics, such as the temptation to "stalk" someone's profile to get a more complete (or distorted) picture of who they are outside of the dating context.

Video Chat and Virtual Dating: The post-pandemic era has witnessed a surge in virtual dating. Video calls have become a popular initial step before deciding to meet in person, offering an additional level of screening. This approach has also presented unique challenges, such as the need to maintain a meaningful connection and interaction through a screen, without the benefit of physical presence and non-verbal cues.

Rise of Specialized Apps: In addition to the well-known giants of online dating, there has been exponential growth in specialized apps catering to specific demographics or interests. For example, there are apps for nature lovers, fitness enthusiasts, specific ethnicities, sexual orientations, or even fans of particular music genres. This specialization can help people find someone with very specific interests but may also limit the diversity of individuals they meet.

Handling Disappointments: In the world of online dating, facing disappointments is inevitable. Whether it's unmet expectations, dates that don't turn into relationships, or relationships that end before they truly begin, learning to manage these moments is crucial. This requires resilience, self-awareness, and the ability not to take things too personally. After all, every interaction can be seen as an opportunity for growth and learning.

Privacy Challenges: Protecting one's privacy is a growing concern in the digital age, and online dating is no exception. From sharing personal details too soon to the risk of scams and catfishing, it's essential to be informed and cautious about how and with whom you share information.

Psychological Impact: Constant exposure to profiles of "perfect people" can impact our self-esteem. Comparing oneself to others is a common trap, leading to questions like "Why don't I get as many 'matches' as my friend?" or "Why don't I seem to have the same results?". These comparisons can create feelings of inadequacy or self-doubt.

The world of online dating is a microcosm that reflects the complexity of the digital era we live in. It combines technology, human emotions, aspirations, and insecurities in an ever-changing context. Furthermore, it represents a convergence between our innate need for connection and our growing dependence on technology as a means to achieve that connection.

On one hand, online dating offers undeniable advantages. The wide range of options, the ability to filter potential partners based on specific criteria, and the opportunity to connect with people outside our immediate social circle are all aspects that have transformed how we build relationships in the 21st century. Additionally, for many people, especially those belonging to specific demographic groups or interest niches, online dating provides a way to find community and build relationships in an environment that previously may have seemed exclusive or limiting.

However, like every coin has its flip side, the digitization of dating has also brought a set of challenges. The abundance of choices can paradoxically make it harder to make a definitive choice. The online representation of ourselves, often filtered and idealized, can create unrealistic expectations and lead to disappointments. The ease with which we can "swipe" through human profiles can, in some cases, lead to the dehumanization of potential partners, reducing them to mere photos and brief descriptions. And, of course, the risk of scams, fraud, and privacy breaches is always lurking.

In conclusion, like any tool, online dating is what we make of it. To successfully navigate this world, it is essential to combine digital prudence with emotional self-awareness. We must recognize that behind every profile is a real person with emotions, hopes, and fears. In the digital age, more than ever, it is crucial to keep humanity at the center of our search for love and connection.

8. Safety First: Tips and Tricks to Ensure Your Safety During Dates

Navigating the world of dating, both online and offline, can be an exciting and rewarding experience. However, ensuring your safety at every stage of the process is crucial. Below are some tips and tricks that every woman should consider to protect herself while exploring the world of dating:

Personal Information: When creating a profile on an online dating platform, it's essential to be cautious about sharing personal details. Avoid including information such as your home address, workplace, or other details that could allow someone to trace you without your consent.

First Meetings in Public Places: When deciding to meet someone for the first time, choose a public place like a café, park, or restaurant. These places are generally safe and allow you to have other people around in case of need.

Inform Someone: Before going out, always inform a friend or family member of the location of the meeting and the expected return time. This ensures that someone knows where you are and can intervene or alert authorities if necessary.

Use Your Own Transportation: Especially for the first few dates, it's advisable to use your own transportation rather than being picked up at home or sharing a car. This gives you more control over the situation and allows you to leave quickly if needed.

Trust Your Instincts: If something doesn't feel right or you feel uncomfortable, trust your instincts. There's nothing wrong with ending a date or a conversation if you don't feel at ease.

Avoid Alcohol and Drugs: Consuming alcohol or drugs can impair your judgment and increase the risk of finding yourself in dangerous situations. If you decide to drink, be mindful of the amount, and never leave your drinks unattended.

Online Research: Before meeting someone, it can be helpful to do a quick online search to ensure there are no reports or suspicious behaviors associated with that person.

Use Safety Apps: Several apps are designed to enhance safety during dates. These apps can send your real-time location to trusted individuals, offer an emergency alarm, or even record audio if necessary.

Plan a Verification Call: Ask a friend to call you at a predetermined time during your date. This provides an opportunity to check that everything is going well and, if necessary, use the call as an excuse to end the encounter.

The key to successfully navigating the world of dating is finding a balance between openness and caution. While it's important to be open to new experiences and people, it's equally fundamental to ensure your safety and well-being in every situation. With proper preparation and by following these tips, you can enjoy the dating process while staying safe.

Keep Your Banking Information Secure: In the digital age, sharing payment details for various services has become common. During dates, especially online ones, you should never share banking or credit card information with someone you've just met. Scammers often pose as sincere individuals in search of love but may have malicious intentions.

Be Cautious About Photo Sharing: Sending or receiving photos may seem like an act of intimacy or trust, but it should be done with caution. Once shared, images can be used in unexpected or unwanted ways. Some individuals may even use them for blackmail.

Beware of Manipulative Behaviors: Not all security threats are physical. Some people may try to manipulate you emotionally or psychologically. Recognize signs of manipulative behaviors, such as gaslighting, and keep your distance from those who attempt to confuse or belittle your experiences.

Check Your Dating App Privacy Settings: Most dating apps have various privacy settings that allow you to control who can see your profile, photos, or recent locations visited. Make sure to understand and use these settings to protect your privacy.

Vaccinations and Sexual Health: Safety isn't just about protection from potential physical or emotional harm. If there may be intimacy involved, it's essential to protect yourself in terms of health. Open communication about sexually transmitted disease testing and understanding the importance of vaccinations, such as the HPV vaccine, is crucial.

Self-Defense Training: While hoping never to use self-defense techniques, being trained in this field can provide greater peace of mind. There are courses specifically designed for women that teach effective and practical defense techniques in various situations.

Clear Expectations: Clear communication about your expectations can prevent misunderstandings that could lead to uncomfortable or potentially dangerous situations. Whether you're seeking a serious relationship or something more casual, being transparent about your intentions can help establish clear boundaries.

Sharing Experiences: If you've had a negative or suspicious experience with someone, consider the opportunity to share it on appropriate platforms or apps, as long as it doesn't compromise your privacy or safety. This can help others be cautious and protect themselves from potentially dangerous individuals.

Beware of Over-sharers: People who excessively share intimate or personal details in the first meeting or early messages may lack appropriate boundaries. This can be a warning sign indicating the need to proceed with caution.

Navigating the dating world requires a combination of open-mindedness, trust, and caution. By always prioritizing your safety, you can explore relationships in a healthy and secure manner.

Red Flags: It's essential to learn to recognize red flags. If someone becomes excessively jealous, possessive, or controlling, or tries to isolate you from your friends or family, these are clear indicators of potentially harmful or abusive behavior.

Location Tracking Apps: There are applications that allow you to share your real-time location with trusted individuals. If you find yourself in a situation where you feel unsafe, these apps can send a distress signal or simply let someone know where you are.

Identity Verification: With the popularity of online dating, it has become common for people to alter their identity. Consider using identity verification services or simply search the person's name on Google to ensure that the provided information matches reality.

Use Technology to Your Advantage: In addition to dating apps, there are numerous devices and applications specifically designed for personal safety. For example, some smartwatches have SOS functions that can be activated in emergency situations.

Balance Heart and Mind: While it's natural to get carried away by the excitement of a new relationship or the thrill of a first date, it's crucial to balance these emotions with rational thinking. Ask questions, listen attentively, and assess whether the person's actions align with their words.

Digital Protection: In addition to safeguarding your personal information, make sure to protect your devices. Using complex passwords, enabling two-factor authentication, and being aware of phishing tactics can prevent situations where your personal information is compromised.

Take Advantage of Reviews: Some online dating platforms offer the opportunity to leave feedback or reviews about users. These can provide valuable information about a potential partner's past behavior.

Avoid Isolation: Even though it might seem romantic to spend all your time with a new flame, maintaining your own habits and relationships is healthy. Friends and family can offer an external perspective on your relationship and help you recognize any worrisome behaviors.

Beware of "Ghosting": "Ghosting," the act of ceasing all communication without explanations, has become a common practice in the modern dating world. While it can be painful, it's important to remember that this behavior often reflects the insecurities of the other person, not your worth.

Remember You Deserve the Best: Finally, every person deserves respect, kindness, and consideration in a relationship. If you start feeling that you have to lower your standards or tolerate behaviors that don't make you feel valued, it may be time to reassess the relationship or encounter.

While the dating world may seem like a minefield of potential pitfalls, entering the game with proper preparation and vigilance allows you to enjoy the journey in search of love or companionship, knowing that you are doing everything possible to protect yourself.

Safety in dating, both online and offline, is not just a precaution but an imperative necessity in the modern era. While technological progress has expanded our possibilities for connection, it has also introduced new challenges that require awareness and readiness. Protecting personal data, being cautious about meeting new people, and the ability to identify warning signs are all essential skills for those venturing into the world of dating.

Dating represents a personal journey, a search for connection and mutual understanding. But to ensure that this journey is enriching and positive, it's essential to prioritize safety. This doesn't mean living in fear or limiting your openness to new experiences; on the contrary, it means having control over your own path, being informed, and prepared.

It's crucial to recognize that every individual has the right to feel safe, respected, and valued in every interaction. This principle should be the cornerstone of every romantic adventure. Additionally, by paying attention to details and listening to your instincts, you can often avoid ending up in unwanted situations. Friends, family, and online communities can serve as safety nets, offering advice, support, and sometimes validation.

However, it's also essential not to let the fear of vulnerability or potential dangers hinder opportunities to form authentic and meaningful connections. Safety in dating should serve as a balance, allowing people to open up and connect with others while maintaining a sense of personal protection and security.

In conclusion, in the complex dance of modern dating, safety should play the role of a constant guide. With the right amount of attention, preparation, and active listening to your own needs and intuitions, you can explore the vast world of dating with confidence, ensuring that your safety always comes first.

9. Chemistry and Compatibility: Recognizing the Difference and the Importance of Both

In the world of dating and relationships, the words "chemistry" and "compatibility" are often used interchangeably, but they represent two distinct and complementary aspects of interpersonal connection.

Chemistry:

1. **Definition:** Chemistry can be described as that initial attraction or intense spark experienced when meeting someone for the first time. It manifests as either physical attraction or an electrifying sense of connection.

2. **Characteristics:** Chemistry tends to be spontaneous and instantaneous. It is based on a guttural or visceral reaction to another person and can develop rapidly.

3. **Positives:** It can act as a powerful catalyst in the early stages of a relationship, helping people connect quickly and grow closer to each other.

4. **Limitations:** Although chemistry is exciting and captivating, it can also be temporary. It does not necessarily guarantee a long-term connection or a successful relationship.

Compatibility:

1. **Definition:** Compatibility pertains to two people's ability to coexist harmoniously over the long term. It is based on shared values, life goals, habits, communication styles, and worldviews.

2. **Characteristics:** Unlike chemistry, which can be immediate, compatibility may take time to fully manifest. It is something that is discovered through extended interactions, deep discussions, and navigating through challenges and conflicts.

3. **Positives:** Strong compatibility can lead to a lasting relationship, providing a stable foundation upon which to build a partnership.

4. **Limitations:** Compatibility alone, without chemistry, may not be enough to sustain a passionate or vibrant relationship. It may lack that "fire" that many people seek in a romantic connection.

The Importance of Both: Both chemistry and compatibility play crucial roles in forming and maintaining successful relationships. While chemistry can attract people to each other and create an initial bond, compatibility is what helps sustain the connection over time, through ups and downs.

Many relationships start with intense chemistry but may face difficulties when insurmountable differences emerge. Similarly, some people may share deep compatibility, but if the initial spark is missing, the relationship may seem flat or lacking in passion.

Many have experienced the thrill of instant attraction, where a glance or a simple touch triggers a cascade of emotions. This is chemistry, an almost magnetic force that draws us toward someone. It's visceral, often uncontrollable, and can stem from various sources: physical attraction, intense emotional connection, or an innate sense of familiarity.

From a biological perspective, chemistry can be seen as our body's response to pheromones—chemical substances released that can influence the behavior of others of the same species. This instinctive response has deep roots in our evolution, geared toward finding a genetically compatible partner.

However, if we relied solely on chemistry, our relationships would be fleeting. The intensity of chemistry tends to wane over time; it's the nature of its fleeting allure. For many, it can become a relentless quest, jumping from one relationship to another in search of that initial spark, only to find it fades quickly.

On the other hand, compatibility manifests in very different ways. Think of all the couples who describe their relationship as "being best friends." This kind of bond comes from a profound mutual understanding. Compatibility is about sharing core values, life goals, and worldviews. And while chemistry may fade, compatibility can actually strengthen over time as people get to know each other better and build a shared history.

Interestingly, our modern society tends to value chemistry more than compatibility. Movies, songs, and novels often glorify the idea of passionate, instant love. Rarely do we hear the story of two people slowly building a relationship through mutual understanding and shared experiences.

But to have a healthy, lasting relationship, it's essential to recognize the importance of both. If we imagine a relationship as a plant, chemistry could be likened to the water that gives life to the plant, while compatibility can be seen as the nurturing soil in which the plant grows. Both are essential for its survival and flourishing.

Awareness of these dynamics can also help navigate relational challenges. For example, in times when chemistry seems to fade, the strength of compatibility can support the couple. And in moments when differences or tensions arise, the memory of the initial chemistry can serve as a reminder of the special bond that exists.

The key lies in balance. Too often, people mistake the absence of chemistry for the absence of love, or the presence of chemistry for deep compatibility. But by recognizing that they are two sides of the same coin, we can have a more complete view of what it truly means to connect with another person.

In addition to what has already been said about chemistry and compatibility, there is much more to explore. For instance, both of these aspects have deep roots in our past experiences and personal beliefs. How we perceive chemistry and compatibility is influenced by our previous relationships, our family of origin, and the models of love we observed when we were young.

Our first model of love generally comes from our parents or caregivers. From them, we learn what it means to love and be loved, but also how to handle conflicts, communicate, and navigate life's challenges. These early learnings can create expectations and patterns in our future romantic relationships. For example, if we saw our parents handle conflicts through dialogue and compromise, we might seek a partner with open and honest communication. On the other hand, if we witnessed conflict-ridden or distant relationships, we might unconsciously repeat these patterns in our own relationships.

Furthermore, our culture and society play a significant role in our perception of chemistry and compatibility. Different cultures have different definitions of what it means to be compatible. In some cultures, compatibility might be seen in terms of family background, social status, education, or religion. In others, it might be more focused on emotional connection and shared passions.

The digital age has also influenced how we perceive chemistry and compatibility. With the advent of online dating, we can now filter potential partners based on a list of preferences. However, while these platforms can help us find people who seem compatible on paper, they cannot predict the chemical spark we may or may not feel when we meet someone in person.

Another interesting point is how chemistry and compatibility interact with our biology. Hormones like oxytocin and vasopressin are released when we feel in love, contributing to that feeling of euphoria and connection. But these hormones tend to level off after the so-called "honeymoon phase," and what often remains is long-term compatibility.

Finally, it's essential to recognize that chemistry and compatibility are not static. They change and evolve over time. A couple might discover new dimensions of their compatibility years after being together, or they might work through issues to strengthen their chemical connection.

A deep understanding of these aspects can enrich our dating and relationship experiences, offering us a more nuanced and comprehensive view of what it truly means to connect with another human being.

Chemistry and compatibility are two fundamental yet distinct elements in the mosaic of a romantic relationship. Chemistry represents that immediate spark, the physical and emotional attraction we often feel toward someone. It's a potent barometer of our initial reactions and can serve as a catalyst to bring us closer to someone. However, it's fickle and, in many cases, temporary. Chemistry can ignite and fade, influenced by a myriad of factors, including life circumstances, moods, and even biology.

Compatibility, on the other hand, is the sum of similarities, differences, and a couple's ability to coexist harmoniously on various levels, such as values, aspirations, lifestyles, and worldviews. While chemistry can be likened to the quick and brilliant fire of a match, compatibility is like the slow-burning but constant ember, providing warmth and light for a longer duration.

Throughout human history, we've seen countless examples of couples who had unmatched chemistry but lacked compatibility. These relationships often burn brightly for a brief period but can quickly extinguish when reality sets in. Similarly, there have been many couples who, while not having an obvious chemistry initially, discovered deep compatibility over time, building lasting and meaningful relationships.

In the modern era, with the increasing complexity of dating and relationships, it's more important than ever to distinguish between these two elements. Recognizing the difference between chemistry and compatibility can help us make more informed and intentional choices in our partners, to look beyond the fleeting and seek what is sustainable. While chemistry can offer unforgettable moments of passion and connection, it is compatibility that provides the opportunity for a deeper and enduring connection.

Ultimately, the key to a successful relationship lies in finding a balance between these two elements. It's the marriage of palpable chemistry and solid compatibility that offers the best chances for lasting love. And while there is no magic formula to guarantee this balance, self-awareness, understanding, and communication are essential tools that can help us navigate this delicate dance between the heart and the mind.

Rejection, in all its forms, is an inevitable reality in the world of dating. It comes in various ways: an unanswered message, a date that doesn't lead to a second meeting, a relationship that ends abruptly. Although it may seem like an unpleasant and disagreeable experience, it's important to approach rejection with a healthy and constructive perspective.

Origins of Rejection

Rejection can have many origins. It can result from external circumstances, such as changes in a person's personal life, or it can stem from a lack of compatibility or attraction. Sometimes, people fear commitment or are not yet ready for a relationship. Other times, individuals simply feel that something is amiss, even if they cannot pinpoint exactly what it is.

Psychological Effects of Rejection

Psychologically, rejection can trigger a range of negative emotions. The rejected person may feel inadequate, undesirable, or dismissed. These feelings can lead to self-doubt, lowered self-esteem, and, in some cases, depression or anxiety.

Tools for Dealing with Rejection

1. **Don't Take It Personally:** It's essential to understand that rejection is not necessarily a reflection of you as an individual. Everyone has their own battles, insecurities, and motivations, and what may seem like rejection may have little to do with you directly.
2. **Reflect on the Situation:** Analyze the experience. Is it possible that you overlooked some signals? Are there lessons to be learned that could help you in the future?
3. **Talk About Your Emotions:** Share your feelings with trusted friends or consider speaking with a professional. Expressing what you feel can help you process the experience.

4. **Boost Your Self-Esteem:** Dedicate time to yourself, learn something new, or indulge in your passions. Remind yourself of your worth.
5. **Accept and Let Go:** One of life's most powerful skills is the ability to accept and move on. Not all encounters or relationships are meant to last, and that's okay.

Looking Beyond Rejection

Overcoming rejection can be a process of personal growth. It can teach you resilience, empathy, and the ability to handle disappointments. It can also provide you with a deeper perspective on what you truly desire in a relationship and what is worth pursuing.

Managing rejection in the context of dating is a challenge that requires a profound understanding of oneself and social dynamics. Often, rejection is perceived as a direct judgment of our worth as individuals. However, once you begin to decode the complexities behind rejection, you can start to see it in a different light.

Rejection Across Cultures

Globally, each culture has its unique perspective on rejection. In some cultures, rejecting or being rejected is seen as a matter of incompatibility rather than a personal defect. Other cultures may emphasize the importance of persistence and view rejection as a mere obstacle. Understanding these cultural differences can provide a refreshing perspective.

Group Dynamics and Rejection

Rejection can also be influenced by group dynamics. For example, in a group where a particular norm or expectation prevails, those who do not conform to that norm may feel excluded or rejected. This can manifest in subtle ways, such as when someone is excluded from a group of friends or not invited to a party.

Personal Growth Through Rejection

Every rejection comes with a lesson. It might teach you something about what you're looking for in a relationship, or it might offer insight into a behavior or habit you might want to change. Many find that, through a series of rejections, they develop a deeper understanding of themselves and their needs in a relationship.

The Role of Technology

In the digital age, the frequency of rejection has exponentially increased. Dating apps allow people to "swipe left" on potential partners with a simple gesture. This ease can lead to an increased sense of rejection. However, it's crucial to remember that in these contexts, decisions are often made quickly, based on limited information, and do not reflect thorough judgment.

Resilience

Being able to face rejection and move forward requires resilience. This ability to bounce back from negative experiences is essential in the world of dating. Resilience is not about ignoring or suppressing feelings of rejection but accepting them, processing them, and using them as a foundation for growth.

The Importance of Self-Compassion

When facing rejection, practicing self-compassion can be extremely beneficial. This means treating yourself with the same kindness, concern, and understanding you would offer to a dear friend. Recognizing that rejection is part of the human condition and that you are not alone in these feelings can help you navigate the experience with greater grace.

The Psychological Aspect of Rejection

The human brain is wired for connection. Since ancient times, being part of a group meant a higher likelihood of survival. That's why rejection can trigger such a deep emotional response: biologically, we are programmed to perceive rejection as a threat to our safety. In an MRI study, scientists found that the same brain areas activated by physical pain are also activated by social rejection. This means that, at a neurological level, the emotional pain of rejection can be comparable to physical pain.

Modern Society and Rejection

In today's society, where public image and social perception play a dominant role, rejection can have even deeper ramifications. Platforms like social media intensify this perception. A lack of "likes" or positive comments can be interpreted as rejection from the larger group, fueling insecurities and doubts.

Rejection and Self-Esteem

The relationship between self-esteem and rejection is complex. Low self-esteem can make a person more sensitive to rejection, while repeated experiences of rejection can further erode one's self-esteem. It's a cycle that can fuel anxiety and depression. That's why having tools and strategies to break this cycle, such as therapy, the support of trusted friends, or self-reflection, is essential.

The Positive Side of Rejection

Although it may seem counterintuitive, there are positive aspects of rejection. For starters, it can act as a filter, helping you understand who is genuinely compatible with you and who is not. Rejection can also be seen as a form of feedback: it can give you clues about behaviors or habits you may want to reconsider. Additionally, facing rejection can strengthen your resilience, preparing you for future challenges.

Different Forms of Rejection

Rejection can manifest in many ways. There's direct rejection, where someone tells you clearly that they are not interested. But there are also subtler forms, such as ghosting, where someone disappears without explanation. Each form of rejection has unique challenges and requires different coping methods.

Rejection and Growth

Every experience of rejection carries the potential for growth. Over time and with reflection, many people find that their most painful experiences of rejection have actually led them to a greater understanding of themselves and what they want in a relationship.

Self-Compassion in Rejection

An essential component of handling rejection is self-compassion. This is the ability to treat oneself with kindness, empathy, and understanding, especially in challenging times like after rejection. Many people tend to be harshly self-critical after experiencing rejection, which can only exacerbate the pain and disappointment. The practice of self-compassion, on the other hand, helps you remember that everyone, regardless of their situation, experiences rejection. You are not alone in this.

Rejection as Part of the Journey

Rejection, while unpleasant, is an inevitable aspect of the journey of love. In fact, even the most charming, intelligent, and successful individuals face rejection. Instead of seeing it as a failure or a judgment of your worth, consider it as a signal guiding you toward a relationship or experience that is better suited for you. Every "no" brings you closer to a meaningful "yes."

The Art of Detachment

Another crucial skill when dealing with rejection is the art of detachment. This doesn't mean suppressing or ignoring your feelings, but rather accepting rejection without letting it define your sense of self or self-esteem. This requires practice and mindfulness, but over time, you can develop resilience that allows you to handle rejection with balance and grace.

Putting Things in Perspective

Remember that rejection is just a moment in the vast arc of your life. While it may feel all-consuming when it occurs, its impact diminishes over time. What may seem devastating today could be a small memory a year from now. By valuing the lessons learned and using rejection as an opportunity for introspection, you can actually emerge from these experiences stronger and wiser.

Creating a Support Network

When facing rejection, it's essential to have a support network to rely on. Friends, family, and mental health professionals can provide listening ears, advice, and comfort. Talking about your experiences and feelings with someone you trust can help you process the pain and disappointment and see things in a different light.

Practicing Rejection

Although it may seem counterintuitive, practicing rejection can actually help build resilience. This might involve putting yourself in situations where rejection is possible, such as asking for a favor or making a proposal. The more you expose yourself to rejection in small doses, the more manageable it becomes when it occurs in more significant contexts like dating.

In summary, while rejection can be painful, it is not insurmountable. With the right mindset, tools, and support, it can become an opportunity for personal growth, self-discovery, and ultimately, for getting closer to a relationship that truly resonates with who you are.

First and foremost, it is crucial to recognize that rejection is not a verdict on your worth as an individual. Just as in many aspects of life, dating is subjective. What one person may not appreciate or desire could be precisely what another person is seeking. Therefore, each rejection is simply a sign that there was not alignment between you and the other person at that particular moment or in that context.

The key, then, lies in the approach to rejection. Self-compassion is fundamental. Instead of falling into self-destructive or self-critical traps, treat yourself with the same kindness and understanding you would offer to a dear friend. This allows you to process rejection in a healthy way and move forward with dignity.

Perspective is another crucial element. Consider rejection as a detour rather than a dead-end. Each experience offers valuable lessons that can inform and enrich your journey. When you view rejection as part of the journey, rather than an insurmountable obstacle, it becomes easier to find the strength and motivation to keep searching.

Finally, surround yourself with a solid support network. Friends, family, and if necessary, mental health professionals can offer an external perspective, comfort, and strategic advice on how to handle rejection and move forward.

In summary, while rejection can be painful, it is not insurmountable. With the right mindset, tools, and support, it can become an opportunity for personal growth, self-discovery, and ultimately, for getting closer to a relationship that truly resonates with who you are.

The Art of Flirting: Techniques and Tips for Authentic Flirting

Flirting is an ancient and subtle art, a dance between two people that expresses interest, attraction, and playfulness. In the context of dating, it's often the first step in establishing a connection. But how can you flirt authentically without appearing forced or insincere? Here are some techniques and tips:

1. **Active Listening:** First and foremost, listen. Flirting isn't just about talking; it's also about listening. Showing genuine interest in what the other person has to say creates a bond. Active listening means being present in the moment, reacting to the other person's words, and demonstrating through body language that you are interested.

2. **Eye Contact:** Eye contact is a powerful form of non-verbal communication. A gaze can convey interest, curiosity, and invitation. Don't stare intensely, but intermittent eye contact can create a sense of intimacy.

3. **Authentic Compliments:** When giving a compliment, make sure it comes from the heart. Praise something that genuinely impresses you about the other person, whether it's their sense of style, laughter, or a personality trait.

4. **Open Body Language:** Open and relaxed body language invites interaction. Smile, tilt your head slightly when listening, and use open hand gestures to show interest.

5. **Light Touch:** If you feel comfortable and sense that the interaction is positive, a light touch on the arm or shoulder can intensify the moment of connection. However, it's essential to respect boundaries and ensure the other person feels comfortable.
6. **Be Yourself:** Sincerity is the key. Don't try to be someone you're not or put on a behavior that doesn't represent you. Authenticity is attractive.
7. **Use Humor:** Laughing together can create a quick and deep bond. Sharing a joke or a laugh about a light-hearted anecdote can ease tension and reveal your playful side.
8. **Ask Questions:** Show your interest by asking open-ended questions, those that can't be answered with a simple "yes" or "no." This stimulates a deeper conversation and shows that you genuinely want to get to know them.
9. **Avoid Heavy Topics:** While there are times when discussing serious topics is appropriate, flirting should be light and playful. Avoid subjects that could be controversial or too deep.
10. **Close with Class:** If you feel the conversation is winding down or you need to leave, conclude the interaction gracefully. Saying "It was a pleasure talking to you" or "I hope to see you again" are sweet and sincere ways to end.

Deep down, we all desire sincere and authentic connections. Flirting with authenticity isn't just about avoiding clichés or behaving transparently; it's about immersing yourself in the art of communicating and connecting on a deeper level.

Get to Know Yourself: Before you can flirt authentically, you need to know what makes you authentic. This means taking time to reflect on your passions, values, and quirks. Only when you know yourself can you present yourself genuinely to others.

Cultivate Empathy: Empathy not only helps you understand others but also creates a deeper connection. When you flirt, try to put yourself in the other person's shoes. This ability allows you to understand their emotions and respond more authentically and connectedly.

Study Non-Verbal Communication: In addition to words, we communicate through gestures, facial expressions, and tone of voice. Developing sensitivity to these signals can help you perceive and respond better during flirting. For example, if the other person crosses their arms or avoids eye contact, they may not feel comfortable. Being attentive to these details allows you to adjust your behavior and make the interaction more enjoyable.

Honesty and Vulnerability: While flirting tends to be light and playful, showing a bit of vulnerability can be a powerful tool for connection. This doesn't mean spilling all your secrets or problems, but sharing small truths about yourself can show that you are genuine.

Mutual Respect: Flirting with authenticity also means respecting others' boundaries. If you sense that the other person is not interested or doesn't feel comfortable, it's essential to respect their feelings and gracefully withdraw.

Practice and Learning: Like any skill, flirting requires practice. Each interaction offers an opportunity to learn and refine your abilities. Pay attention to what works and what doesn't, and use every experience as a growth opportunity.

Maintain a Sense of Curiosity: Flirting is, in many ways, an exploration. It's about discovering new people, new stories, and new experiences. Maintaining a sense of curiosity helps you stay open and interested, making each interaction fresh and lively.

The Art of Flirting: Not Just Techniques, but a Path to Authenticity and Connection

Flirting is not just a series of techniques to learn; it's a journey toward greater authenticity and connection. Through practice, reflection, and, above all, being open to your true self and others, flirting can become not only a game but also a means to create deeper and more meaningful relationships.

Active Listening: An essential component of authentic flirting is active listening. When you interact with someone, you need to genuinely pay attention to what they are saying, without mentally formulating your response while they talk. Active listening allows you not only to truly understand the other person but also to show that you care about them as an individual. This kind of attention can create a deep and meaningful connection in a short amount of time.

Use of Humor: Humor is a powerful tool in flirting. Not only does it lighten the atmosphere, but laughing together can create a sense of camaraderie and intimacy. However, it's important to be mindful of the type of humor you use. Humor that targets others or can be offensive is not only inauthentic but can also create barriers rather than connections.

Awareness of Cultural Differences: In an increasingly globalized world, you may find yourself flirting with people from different cultures than your own. It's crucial to be aware of cultural differences and the various norms regarding flirting and courtesy. Something that might be considered appropriate in your culture may not be so in another.

Technology as a Tool: With the advent of smartphones and social media, flirting has taken many new forms. While emojis, gifs, and messages can simplify the expression of interest or affection, it's essential to remember that digital communication can easily lead to misunderstandings. It's always a good idea to be clear in your intentions and try to keep communication as authentic as possible, even in a digital format.

Feedback and Adaptability: Observe the reactions of the person you're flirting with. If they seem comfortable and responsive, you're likely heading in the right direction. However, if they appear to withdraw or become nervous, it may be time to change your approach or gracefully step back. Being able to read and adapt to others' reactions is a fundamental skill in the art of flirting.

Authenticity vs. Role-playing: While flirting often involves a degree of role-playing or exaggeration, it's crucial to find a balance. You can present your best self, but without distorting who you truly are. The goal should always be to let your true personality shine through, rather than a fictional version of yourself.

Valuing Each Other's Individuality: Every individual is unique, with their own stories, experiences, and worldviews. Celebrating these differences can not only help you connect on a deeper level but also learn and grow as an individual. Through flirting, you can discover new perspectives and ways of seeing the world, enriching your understanding of others and yourself.

Finally, while flirting can have many different goals, from forming a friendship to starting a romantic relationship, the essence remains the same: the connection between two individuals. Through authenticity, understanding, and vulnerability, flirting can become a bridge between two people, allowing them to share, even if just for a moment, a piece of their souls.

Body Language: One of the most crucial aspects of authentic flirting involves body language. Every gesture, glance, or touch can communicate more than a thousand words. Prolonged eye contact, for instance, can indicate interest and attraction, while leaning in towards someone can suggest attentiveness and curiosity. Conversely, a closed-off body, with crossed arms or avoiding eye contact, may signal disinterest or discomfort.

Voice and Tone: The tone of your voice, speaking rhythm, and intonation can all play a fundamental role in flirting. A sweet and relaxed voice can create an atmosphere of comfort and intimacy, while a playful and light tone can stimulate laughter and enjoyment. It's essential to be aware of how you use your voice and the message you're sending.

Timing and Pace: Flirting is not a race. Taking the time to get to know each other, establish a connection, and appreciate small moments can make the interaction deeper and more meaningful. Patience and the ability to listen are essential. Forcing things or rushing can often disrupt the natural flow of conversation and create tension.

Value of Mystery: While being authentic, maintaining a certain level of mystery can make flirting more exciting. This doesn't mean hiding aspects of yourself or being dishonest but rather not revealing everything right away. Allowing room for curiosity and anticipation can often fuel interest.

Mutual Respect: Even during flirting, respect for the other individual is crucial. This means respecting their boundaries, actively listening to their concerns and desires, and not making premature assumptions or judgments. Flirting should be a mutual path where both parties feel seen, heard, and appreciated.

Empathy and Understanding: Trying to put yourself in the other person's shoes, understanding their emotions and feelings, is essential. Empathy can help create a deeper bond and navigate more consciously through the art of flirting.

Setting Boundaries: Even in flirting, it's essential to have clear boundaries and communicate them. This can refer to how comfortable you are sharing personal information, how far you want the conversation to go, and how you want it to be treated. Being clear about your boundaries not only protects your well-being but also shows the other person that you respect yourself.

Popular Culture and Flirting: We live in an era where popular culture has a significant influence on how we perceive and interpret flirting. Movies, TV series, songs, and even memes provide us with countless examples of what it means to flirt. However, it's important to remember that these are often exaggerated or idealized for entertainment. Taking these examples literally can lead to unrealistic expectations and misunderstandings.

The practice of flirting, a seductive dance as ancient as humanity itself, has long been seen as an art to perfect. At the heart of this intricate ballet of gestures, words, and glances lies a deep human desire for connection, recognition, and intimacy with others. But what makes flirting so captivating and, at times, so complex is that it intersects with many dynamics: sincerity and playfulness, attraction and reticence, boldness and discretion.

Authenticity in flirting is essential because it is based on a true understanding of oneself and a desire to genuinely present oneself to the other person. It's not about wearing a mask or playing a role but expressing oneself sincerely while considering one's emotions and desires, as well as those of the other person. However, this doesn't mean there's no room for mystery and play; on the contrary, ambiguity and the unspoken are often what fuels attraction in flirting.

The techniques and tips for successful flirting, such as body language and vocal tone, are important, but what truly matters is the awareness with which they are used. This awareness arises from self-knowledge, an understanding of one's motivations, and respect for others. In an era dominated by popular culture, where flirting is often depicted in idealized or stereotyped ways, it is essential to reflect critically on what we see and hear, remembering that each individual and each interaction is unique.

Furthermore, at every stage of flirting, mutual respect must be the foundation. This means recognizing and honoring the boundaries of others, as well as communicating your own clearly. Safety and comfort are essential for building a sincere and deep connection.

In conclusion, the art of flirting is a journey of self-discovery and connection with others. It's not just about techniques or tricks but a profound sense of authenticity, empathy, and respect. And while the landscape of dating and relationships may change over time, the quest for connection, recognition, and love remains universal. To master the art of flirting, it's essential to look within, be present in the moment, and approach others with curiosity, openness, and kindness.

12. The Importance of Independence: Maintaining Your Individuality While Seeking a Relationship

Many people, consciously or not, approach the world of dating with the hope of finding someone who can complete them. This notion, popularized by movies, songs, and romantic stories, suggests that we are incomplete without another. However, it's essential to understand that a partner should never "complete" you but rather "complement" you.

Independence, understood as the ability to maintain and value your own individuality, is crucial not only for your personal well-being but also for building healthy and mutually respectful relationships. Here's why:

1. **Self-Realization:** First and foremost, recognizing and cultivating your own identity allows you to have a clear vision of what you desire and what you bring into a relationship. This process of self-realization helps define your values, interests, and goals, which are essential for establishing compatibility with a potential partner.

2. **Preventing Emotional Dependency:** Independence reduces the risk of emotional dependency, where one partner becomes excessively reliant on the other for their emotional well-being. This type of relationship often leads to power imbalances and can limit the personal growth of both partners.

3. **Promoting Mutual Growth:** In a relationship where both partners are independent, there's more room for mutual growth. Both can learn from each other, encourage each other's passions and interests, and build a relationship based on understanding and mutual respect.

4. **Enhancing Relationship Quality:** Relationships in which both partners maintain their individuality are generally more balanced and satisfying. Each person enters the relationship as a complete individual, meaning

the relationship is an addition to their life rather than a necessity.

5. **Preserving Identity:** Maintaining your independence ensures that you don't lose sight of who you truly are. It's easy, especially in the early stages of a relationship, to become completely absorbed in the partner and the world you share. However, it's crucial to remember to make space for yourself.

6. **Boosting Self-Esteem:** Recognizing and appreciating your individuality strengthens self-esteem. When you are self-assured and know your worth, you are less likely to tolerate behaviors and situations that don't reflect your value.

Maintaining Your Individuality and Independence: This doesn't mean avoiding emotional connection or limiting the depth of intimacy in a relationship. Instead, it means balancing closeness with self-sufficiency, ensuring that while sharing life with someone, you don't lose sight of your own identity.

Balancing Individuality and Sharing: In every relationship, there's a push and pull dynamic between wanting to be close and wanting to maintain some distance. This can be seen as an interaction between independence and interdependence. The key is to find a healthy balance between the two. For example, two individuals may have separate hobbies and spend time with different groups of friends, but they also come together to share experiences, stories, and joint activities.

Respect for Autonomy: In many cultures, there's a growing understanding of the importance of autonomy within a relationship. Respecting your partner's autonomy means recognizing that, even though they are part of your life, they have the right to their own choices, experiences, and paths of growth. This respect is crucial to prevent a relationship from becoming suffocating or limiting.

Impact on Mental Health: The ability to maintain your independence also has significant implications for mental health. People who effectively balance their independence with connection in a relationship tend to show lower levels of anxiety and depression. Furthermore, feeling that you have a degree of control and autonomy in your life can help reduce stress and improve overall well-being.

Preventing Resentment: When you lose sight of your independence in a relationship, subtle resentment can emerge. This can stem from feeling trapped or having sacrificed too much of yourself. On the contrary, maintaining healthy individuality can prevent the accumulation of these negative feelings.

Promoting Individual Growth: A person who maintains their individuality is often more inclined to pursue opportunities for personal growth, whether it's education, professional development, or personal exploration. This, in turn, can bring new energy and perspectives into the relationship.

Creating Separate Spaces: It's not just about keeping distinct interests or hobbies; it's also about recognizing the importance of having separate physical and temporal spaces. These can be moments of tranquility, reflection, or relaxation away from the pressures and expectations of the relationship.

Valuing Differences: One of the wonders of relationships is that they allow two distinct individuals to come together. By maintaining and celebrating these differences, rather than trying to "merge" into one entity, you enrich the fabric of the relationship.

Independence extends beyond keeping separate interests and hobbies. It also involves how you perceive yourself, your decisions, and how you handle conflicts and challenges within the relationship.

Financial Independence: One fundamental aspect of independence is financial freedom. Although couples often choose to merge their finances, having some autonomy in this area can be liberating. It's not just about earning and spending money but also making financial choices, such as investments, without always needing to consult your partner. This autonomy can also reduce potential money-related conflicts within the relationship.

Emotional Independence: Maintaining emotional independence means being able to manage your emotions and moods without overly depending on your partner for comfort or validation. This doesn't mean avoiding emotional support but possessing the tools and resilience to face challenges authoritatively.

Self-Esteem and Validation: Deriving self-esteem from personal achievements and values, rather than the relationship, is crucial. This approach allows you not to depend too much on your partner for validation and affirmation, reducing the risk of developing dependent dynamics.

Conflict Management: When two individuals maintain their independence, they are often better equipped to handle conflicts constructively. This is because, with a clear understanding of themselves, they can communicate their needs and boundaries clearly without losing sight of their priorities.

Independent Growth: Even within a relationship, personal growth continues. And this growth can occur both parallel to the partner and independently. This may include learning new skills, expanding cultural horizons, or spiritual development.

Diversity as Strength: When each individual brings a different set of experiences, knowledge, and skills into the relationship, the couple as a whole can benefit from a broader range of resources. This diversity, stemming from each person's independence, can serve as a source of strength and resilience for the couple.

Learning to Say No: Independence also means learning to say "no" when necessary. Whether it's protecting your time, personal space, or values, having the ability to set boundaries is essential for maintaining a healthy sense of self within the relationship.

Maintaining your independence in a relationship is not an easy task. It requires awareness, commitment, and sometimes the courage to face resistance or misunderstandings. However, the efforts put into this direction will not only strengthen your sense of self but also enrich the relationship, making it more balanced, resilient, and satisfying.

In conclusion, independence within a relationship is not a barrier between partners but rather a stable platform on which both can build a strong and lasting bond.

The Fundamental Foundation: Independence provides a solid foundation, as it's an expression of maturity and self-realization. This foundation allows entering a relationship not out of dependency or necessity but out of authentic and conscious choice because you want to share your life with another person while maintaining your individuality.

A Sign of Relational Health: Contrary to what popular culture might suggest, independence is not a sign of detachment or coldness. It's a sign of relational health. A relationship in which both partners are independent is often characterized by a more balanced power dynamic, fewer conflicts related to control dynamics, and a greater ability to handle external challenges.

Preserving Uniqueness: Independence allows each individual to preserve and nurture what makes them unique. This uniqueness enriches the relationship, introducing new perspectives, experiences, and ways of addressing issues.

Avoiding Codependency: Maintaining healthy independence helps avoid traps like codependency, where one or both partners overly depend on each other for their self-esteem, emotional well-being, or financial stability. Codependent relationships can become toxic and limit the potential for individual and couple growth.

Self-Sufficiency: Being able to rely on oneself in various aspects of life provides internal security that can reduce anxiety and stress within a relationship. This self-sufficiency, whether emotional, financial, or in terms of problem-solving abilities, means that partners can support each other without overly burdening one another.

In summary, independence within a relationship represents the ability to maintain your own space and identity while deeply connecting and engaging with another individual. This balance between individuality and connection is the key to building a healthy, fulfilling, and resilient relationship. Independent individuals can enrich their

relationships with depth, substance, and a range of experiences that make every interaction more meaningful and every shared moment more precious.

13. Dealing with Social Pressure: • How to handle the expectations of friends, family, and society.

Social pressure is an omnipresent element in the lives of many, especially when it comes to the delicate world of dating and relationships. We live in a society that often has well-defined expectations for how we should lead our love lives, and these standards can vary depending on culture, family background, or the social group we find ourselves in. This pressure can manifest in various ways, from invasive questions about our partners to curiosity about why we're still single, or expectations about when we should "settle down." Here's how you can handle it:

1. **Recognize and Define Your Own Expectations:** First and foremost, it's essential to have clarity about what you truly desire, independent of external expectations. This requires deep introspection and honest self-dialogue. Ask yourself, "What do I genuinely want for myself in a relationship? What does a fulfilling and authentic relationship mean to me?"

2. **Strong Sense of Self-Esteem:** Cultivating robust self-esteem can serve as a shield against external pressures. If you feel confident in your

path and choices, it will be easier to remain uninfluenced by others' opinions.

3. **Open Communication:** If someone, whether a friend, family member, or acquaintance, offers unsolicited opinions about your love life, it's important to communicate openly and honestly. Explain gently that, while you appreciate their concern, your love life is a personal matter.

4. **Build a Support System:** Surround yourself with understanding friends and family who respect your choices and support you regardless of social pressures. These people can be a refuge when you feel overwhelmed or frustrated by external expectations.

5. **Set Boundaries:** It's crucial to establish clear boundaries with those who attempt to interfere or pass judgment on your personal life. This might mean changing the subject, spending less time with particularly intrusive individuals, or, in extreme cases, distancing yourself from toxic relationships.

6. **Remember Every Path Is Unique:** There's no pre-set "timeline" for dating, love, or marriage. Every individual has their own pace and unique path in life, and what works for one person may not work for another.

7. **Education and Empathy:** Sometimes, people may not realize the harm they can cause with their comments or expectations. In these cases, it can be helpful to gently educate these individuals, explaining how you feel and asking them to be more understanding.

8. **Reflection and Personal Growth:** Use every comment or criticism as an opportunity to reflect and grow. Ask yourself if there's truth in what's being said and what you can learn from it.

Dealing with social pressure isn't just about how you feel in the context of dating; it's about how you navigate the world while maintaining authenticity and self-awareness. Society, with its constant media messages, daily conversations, and even advertisements, often sets "standards" for how we should live, love, and relate. The challenge lies not only in recognizing these pressures but also in deciding how to respond to them.

When it comes to social pressure, this also refers to the influence of social media. We live in an era where our love life, or lack thereof, can be constantly under the spotlight. Platforms like Instagram, Facebook, and TikTok often show only the highlights of people's lives, creating a distorted image of reality. Continually seeing images of seemingly perfect couples or reading about idealized love stories can intensify the feeling of being "out of place" if you don't conform to these models.

Furthermore, popular culture and movies have long fueled certain narratives about love and relationships. From romantic comedies to TV shows, there is often an idea of "happily ever after," where people find love in picturesque circumstances, and everything ends with a happy ending. These stories can lead to believing that if one's own experience doesn't align with these models, then something is wrong.

Cultural traditions and family beliefs also play a significant role. In some cultures, there is a strong emphasis on the need to find a partner by a certain age or on starting a family. These expectations may come from past generations and may be rooted in cultural values or practical concerns, such as carrying on the family line or caring for elderly parents.

Added to this is peer pressure. As friends begin to settle down, get married, or have children, it may seem like everyone is following a predetermined path while you are left behind. Social events, such as weddings or baptisms, can become sources of anxiety as they may lead to questions about your relationship status or why you are still single.

Finally, there is internal pressure, that inner voice influenced by all external factors, beginning to doubt and question your choices. You might start wondering if you are too picky, if there are unrealistic expectations, or if you are simply missing the "love train."

However, it is crucial to remember that each individual is unique. Everyone's life has a different pace, and what works for one person may not work for another. Comparing your life to that of others can only lead to frustration and dissatisfaction. Facing social pressure also means recognizing these unique aspects and embracing your own path, even if it diverges from the norm.

Understanding and accepting your individuality can become a powerful tool in dealing with social pressure. When you are firmly anchored in your sense of identity and values, external echoes of expectations become less overpowering. But how do you get to this point?

The importance of self-dialogue: The most enduring and influential relationship we will have in our lives is the one with ourselves. Bringing awareness to our internal dialogues can reveal how much we are influenced by external expectations. Asking questions like "Do I really want this for myself, or am I doing it because it's expected of me?" can help untangle your true desires from imposed ones.

Surrounding yourself with positive influences: While it's impossible to completely avoid exposure to social pressures, you can control to some extent the immediate influences. Surrounding yourself with people who value your individuality and support your decisions can make a difference. These individuals can serve as "anchors" in times of doubt and uncertainty.

The art of reflection and meditation: Creating space for personal reflection, whether through meditation, journaling, or simply spending time alone in nature, can offer a break from relentless social expectations.

These moments provide an opportunity to connect with your inner self and realign your goals and desires.

Educating yourself: Understanding the origins of social expectations can offer perspective on why they exist and help you put them into context. Reading and learning about social dynamics, gender roles, and relationships can provide greater understanding and a different perspective on the pressures you feel.

The practice of gratitude: Focusing on what you have, rather than on what's missing or what society says you should have, can transform your perception of your own life. The practice of gratitude can bring a sense of fullness and abundance, reducing feelings of lack or inadequacy.

Seeking professional support: Sometimes, social pressures can become overwhelming to the point where they affect your mental health. In such cases, seeking the support of a professional, such as a therapist or counselor, who can provide tools and techniques to address and manage these pressures, can be helpful.

Flexibility and adaptation: Finally, it's worth noting that life is constantly evolving. What society values or deems important today may change tomorrow. Having the flexibility to adapt and the resilience to endure during challenging times are invaluable qualities.

Encouraging yourself to look beyond external expectations and embracing your unique path can not only offer a sense of liberation but also lead to a more authentic and fulfilling life.

Facing social pressure is not an easy task, but it is crucial for living an authentic and fulfilled life. Society, with its expectations and norms, can often deeply influence our perception of success, happiness, and fulfillment. However, the key is to remember that these external expectations are often the result of cultural, historical, and social conventions that have evolved over time and do not necessarily represent the "truth" or the "right way" to live.

Comparison is one of the biggest challenges that social pressure brings with it. Comparing yourself to others, their achievements, lifestyles, or even their relationship choices can cause insecurity and doubt. However, each individual is unique, with their own life trajectory, challenges, joys, and pains. What may work or bring happiness to one person may not have the same effect on another. It is essential to remember that our uniqueness is what makes us special.

Social pressures often stem from generations of beliefs and practices that may no longer be relevant in the modern world. The freedom to choose your own path, regardless of external expectations, is an act of courage. But the more you practice assertiveness in the face of these pressures, the more you strengthen your self-esteem and reaffirm your self-worth.

Furthermore, having a robust support system is crucial. Friends, family, or professionals who understand and support your vision of life can serve as pillars of strength and reminders that you are not alone on your journey. Solidarity can often provide a refreshing perspective.

In conclusion, facing and overcoming social pressure is a journey that requires awareness, determination, and support. It involves finding your balance between being true to yourself and navigating a world filled with expectations. However, with the right tools and an open mindset, it is possible to live a life that truly reflects who you are, rather than what society expects you to be. And on this journey of authenticity, you can find a deep sense of peace, fulfillment, and true success.

14.   Personal Growth Through Dating:

- How dating can help you grow as an individual.

Dating, beyond the mere quest for a partner, is a journey of self-discovery and personal growth. Exploring the world of dating can unveil many truths about oneself, offer unexpected lessons, and provide opportunities for maturation. Here's how dating can catalyze personal growth.

1. **Enhancing Self-Awareness**: Dating puts you in situations where you must express your expectations, desires, and boundaries. Reflecting on what you want in a partner and a relationship can teach you a lot about yourself and your life priorities.

2. **Learning Empathy and Understanding**: Meeting and connecting with different people provides you with insights into others' stories and experiences. This can enhance your capacity for empathy, understanding, and tolerance.

3. **Developing Communication Skills**: Effective communication is essential for successful dating. You learn to express your thoughts, feelings, and needs in ways that are clear and respectful while also listening and understanding your partner's.

4. **Facing Challenges and Building Resilience**: Not all dates or relationships will succeed. These experiences, both positive and negative, teach you to handle disappointments, rejections, and conflicts. This resilience benefits you in many other areas of life.

5. **Reevaluating Values and Beliefs**: Meeting people with diverse perspectives, values, and beliefs can prompt you to reflect and sometimes reassess your own convictions. It can broaden your mind and make you more open and accepting.

6. **Learning the Importance of Independence**: While dating often involves connecting with others, it can also underscore the importance of being comfortable with yourself and having an independent and fulfilling life.

7. **Developing Introspective Skills**: Reflecting on dating experiences, reactions, and associated feelings provides you with opportunities to become more introspective. This introspection can be a powerful tool for growth.

8. **Cultivating Patience and Optimism**: Finding the right partner may take time. Dating teaches you patience, optimism, and confidence that things can turn out well, even if they don't seem that way at a given moment.

Personal growth through dating is not a new concept but is deeply rooted in the human experience. Dating, in all its nuances, can serve as a prism through which we see ourselves in new lights and contexts.

- **Boosting Self-Esteem**: As you explore the dating world, it's natural to encounter compliments and criticisms. These experiences can help you develop a balanced view of yourself. Receiving praise or compliments can strengthen your self-esteem, while critiques or rejections offer opportunities for self-improvement without letting them bring you down.

- **Fostering a Growth Mindset**: Your mindset toward dating can profoundly influence your approach to life. Viewing dating as a learning opportunity fosters a growth mindset. This allows you to see challenges as opportunities rather than insurmountable obstacles.

- **Navigating Vulnerability**: Opening up to someone on a date, sharing your fears, dreams, and desires, can be a profoundly vulnerable experience. These experiences teach you the importance of vulnerability in intimacy and help you become braver in showing your true self.

- **Managing Loneliness**: Not all dates lead to lasting relationships. There are times when you may feel alone or crave a deeper connection. Learning to manage and embrace loneliness can help you develop a healthier relationship with yourself.

- **Valuing Diversity**: You meet people from different cultural, social, and personal backgrounds while dating. This diversity can expand your worldview and help you understand and appreciate individual differences.

- **Defining Boundaries**: Through dating, you gain a better understanding of what makes you comfortable and what doesn't. This awareness helps you establish and communicate your boundaries, promoting healthier relationships.

- **Improving Decision-Making Skills**: Selecting a partner, deciding where to go on a date, or when to advance a relationship all require reflection and discernment. These choices offer you the opportunity to refine your decision-making skills.

- **Flexibility and Adaptability**: Things don't always go as planned. Perhaps your date is late, or the chosen restaurant is closed. These minor disruptions teach you to be flexible and adapt to changes.

Overall, every dating experience, whether positive or negative, offers you a lens through which you can see yourself and the world in new and illuminating ways. It's a continuous journey of self-discovery, introspection, and, above all, growth.

- **Emotional Maturation**: One of the most profound lessons that dating can offer is emotional maturation. Emotions such as jealousy, insecurity, or happiness become more palpable when interacting with a potential partner. Learning to navigate and manage these emotions is fundamental for sustainable personal growth.

- **Empathy Development**: When faced with situations where your partner has conflicting needs or feelings, you learn the importance of putting yourself in their shoes. This ability to understand and share another person's feelings is essential not only in a relationship but also in everyday interactions.

- **The Art of Patience**: Not all relationships take off immediately; some require time and patience. Waiting for a relationship to develop naturally teaches the virtue of patience and the understanding that precious things in life often require time.

The Importance of Self-Reflection: Dating often provides you with a mirror in which to reflect. Whether it's a behavior you don't like in yourself or a revelation about what you truly desire, dating urges you to analyze yourself on a deeper level.

Resilience in the Face of Challenges: Not every date or relationship goes as planned. There can be heartbreak, misunderstandings, and disappointments. However, the ability to bounce back and try again armed with wisdom and understanding is a testament to human resilience.

Acquiring Listening Skills: A crucial aspect of dating is genuinely listening to your partner. This not only enhances the quality of the relationship but also hones your listening skills, making you more attentive and present in conversations.

Understanding Different Communication Styles: People communicate in different ways. Some may be direct, while others prefer subtle cues. Recognizing and adapting to different communication styles is a skill you can refine through dating.

Prioritization Assessment: Often, dating confronts you with decisions that concern your priorities. Whether it's choosing between time spent with a partner or friends, or understanding how important a career is compared to your love life, dating compels you to examine and sometimes redefine your priorities.

Appreciating Solitude: Despite dating being focused on connecting with others, it also teaches you to value time spent alone. This time can be used for personal reflection, meditation, or simply relaxation.

On the path of dating, every interaction and reflective moment contributes to your personal growth. This journey, with all its ups and downs, is an invaluable opportunity to become the best version of yourself.

Personal Growth through Dating is a multifaceted and profoundly enriching process. Many people enter the dating world with the primary goal of finding a partner but soon discover that the journey itself offers valuable life lessons. Every interaction, every emotion experienced, and every challenge faced during dating contributes to shaping and enriching the individual, helping them develop greater self-awareness and understanding of their relationships with others.

First and foremost, dating can serve as a magnifying glass on our vulnerabilities and strengths. Whether it's insecurities that surface when comparing ourselves to a potential partner or the joy we feel when a connection is authentic, dating provides us with ongoing feedback on our areas of growth. This feedback, though sometimes painful, is essential for our personal development as it enables us to confront and overcome our fears, biases, and insecurities.

Additionally, dating often challenges us to develop effective communication skills. Communication is the key to any successful relationship, and through dating, we learn the importance of expressing our feelings, actively listening, and resolving conflicts constructively. These skills, once acquired, are transferable to all areas of our lives, improving not only our romantic relationships but also our family, friendships, and professional interactions.

Another crucial aspect of personal growth through dating is the opportunity to reflect on our priorities and values. While seeking a partner who aligns with our ideals and life goals, we are often prompted to reflect on the qualities we deem important, the type of relationship we desire, and the life goals we want to pursue. This process of reflection can lead to greater clarity and understanding of what we want from life.

Finally, dating teaches us the importance of resilience. Not every date or relationship has a positive outcome, and facing disappointments, heartbreaks, or rejections requires great inner strength. However, overcoming these challenges makes us stronger, wiser, and better equipped to face future adversities.

In summary, while dating is often seen as a means to find love, it also represents an unparalleled opportunity for personal growth and development. Through the joys and challenges of dating, we are able to discover more about ourselves, develop vital skills, and become more complete and fulfilled individuals.

15. The Importance of Me Time: Finding a Balance Between Seeking a Relationship and Self-Care.

The importance of me time in the pursuit and management of a relationship is crucial to maintain a sense of balance and well-being in one's life. In an era where we are continuously connected and bombarded with various commitments, it becomes increasingly vital to recognize the value of dedicating moments to ourselves.

The desire for a romantic relationship is innate in many of us. Yet, as we strive to connect with others, we often forget to nurture the most important relationship: the one with ourselves. This inner bond is fundamental for our mental, emotional, and physical health. Self-care is not an act of selfishness but rather a necessity for living a balanced and fulfilling life.

When we allocate time for ourselves, we not only recharge but also boost our self-esteem, which, in turn, enhances the quality of our external relationships. A person at peace with themselves, understanding and accepting their needs and desires, is more likely to establish authentic and deep connections with others.

Furthermore, the constant pursuit of a relationship can become exhausting and create stress. If we exclusively focus on the goal of finding a partner, we risk losing sight of who we truly are and what we genuinely want from life and relationships. This can lead to rushed relationships or unhealthy compromises.

On the other hand, taking time for oneself allows for reflection on personal experiences, learning from mistakes, and growing as an individual. It could involve practicing meditation, dedicating time to a hobby, reading a book, or simply taking a solitary walk. These moments are precious because they provide spaces for introspection, necessary to better understand our emotions, aspirations, and fears.

Finding a balance between seeking a relationship and taking care of oneself also means learning to establish healthy boundaries. If we are in a relationship, it is crucial to have moments for ourselves, to cultivate personal passions, and to maintain a degree of independence. This autonomy not only strengthens our individuality but also enriches the relationship, as both partners bring unique experiences, thoughts, and emotions into it.

In conclusion, while relationships with others are an essential component of human life, it is equally crucial to cultivate the relationship with oneself. Striking a balance between these two spheres of life ensures a more harmonious and fulfilling existence. As an ancient proverb goes, "You cannot pour from an empty cup." Taking care of oneself ensures that we always have something to offer, both to ourselves and to others.

16. Recognizing Signs of a Toxic Relationship: Red Flags to Watch For and How to Exit a Harmful Situation.

Recognizing signs of a toxic relationship is essential to protect one's physical, emotional, and psychological well-being. Toxic relationships can manifest in various ways, and unfortunately, many people remain trapped in these situations because they do not recognize or deny the red flags.

Red Flags to Watch For:

1. Controlling Behavior: A toxic partner often seeks to control every aspect of the other person's life, from small daily decisions to significant life moments.

2. Extreme Jealousy: While some degree of jealousy can be natural in a relationship,

extreme jealousy that leads to possessive or accusatory behaviors is a clear alarm.

3. Unhealthy Communication: A toxic partner may avoid open communication, resort to insults, yelling, or conversely, use silence as punishment.

4. Emotional Manipulation: This can include tactics like blame-shifting, threats, or using pity to get what they want.

5. Isolation: A toxic partner might try to isolate the other person from friends, family, or other forms of external support.

6. Lack of Respect: This can manifest through words or actions that diminish the other partner.

7. Physical or Emotional Abuse: Any form of violence, whether physical or verbal, is an unequivocal sign of a toxic relationship.

8. Excessive Dependency: If one partner excessively relies on the other to fulfill all their emotional or physical needs, it can indicate an unhealthy balance.

9. Lack of Support: In a healthy relationship, both partners support each other. If one partner consistently devalues the other's goals or dreams, it's a concerning sign.

10.   Dishonesty and Lack of Trust: Trust is the foundation of every healthy relationship. Lies, deceit, or secrets can quickly erode this crucial milestone.

How to Exit a Harmful Situation:

1. Recognize the Problem: The first step in leaving a toxic relationship is recognizing that the situation is not healthy.

2. Seek External Support: Talk to friends, family, or professionals who can offer an external perspective and support during this challenging time.

3. Set Clear Boundaries: Decide what behaviors are unacceptable and communicate these boundaries to your partner.

4. Make a Plan: If you decide to leave the relationship, it's essential to have a plan on how to do so, especially if there are concerns about your safety.

5. Prioritize Your Safety: In some situations, especially in cases of abuse, involving law enforcement or seeking refuge at a domestic violence shelter may be necessary.

6. Counseling and Therapy: Therapy can provide tools and resources to help overcome the trauma of a toxic relationship and build healthier relationships in the future.

Recognizing a Toxic Relationship: Identifying a toxic relationship can be challenging, especially when emotions, affection, and sometimes shared history can cloud our judgment. Love and affection can make us rationalize or downplay behaviors that, when observed objectively, are clearly harmful.

Factors of Confusion and Self-Justification: Many times, people in toxic relationships might find themselves thinking, "He/she doesn't always do this" or "Sometimes, he/she can be really sweet." These moments of intermittent kindness, combined with periods of abuse, create a cycle that can confuse and trap the victim in a spiral of hope and disillusionment.

The Impact of Time: Over time, a person may become desensitized to or normalize certain toxic behaviors. What was initially unacceptable gradually becomes tolerated, progressively lowering the standard of what is considered acceptable.

The Role of Self-Esteem: Low self-esteem can make a person more vulnerable to toxic relationships.

They may feel they don't deserve better or fear they won't find another partner who accepts them. This insecurity can provide fertile ground for a manipulative or abusive partner.

The Influence of the Surrounding Environment: Sometimes, society, culture, or the community may downplay or justify toxic behaviors. Phrases like "that's just how men are" or "women are simply emotional" can perpetuate harmful stereotypes and normalize unacceptable behaviors.

Impact on Mental and Physical Health: Being in a toxic relationship can have serious repercussions on mental and physical health. Anxiety, depression, eating disorders, and sleep disturbances are just some potential consequences. The ongoing stress of living in a stressful situation can also lead to physical issues such as headaches, digestive problems, and a reduced ability to fight illnesses due to chronic stress.

The Importance of Education: Educating oneself about toxic signs and behaviors is crucial. This can help recognize early signs before they become severe. Seminars, workshops, and books can offer valuable guidance.

The Power of a Support Network: Although it may seem challenging, sharing one's experiences with trusted individuals can provide an external perspective. Friends and family can recognize signs of a toxic relationship before the person involved does and can offer valuable support.

Finally, it is crucial to remember that every individual deserves respect, love, and care in a relationship. If these elements are missing or are obscured by harmful behaviors, it may be time to reconsider the relationship and seek external support.

Recognizing Signs of a Toxic Relationship is Essential for Individual Well-Being and Self-Esteem: However, confronting and accepting that one may be involved in such a relationship can be difficult and painful. A detailed understanding of what makes a relationship harmful is the first step in protecting oneself.

1. **Cyclical Behavior:** One of the hallmark features of toxic relationships is their cyclic nature. Moments of tension, followed by an incident (often harmful behavior), and then a honeymoon phase where everything seems to return to normal. This cycle can repeat many times, making it difficult for the victim to recognize toxicity or break the cycle.

2. **Normalization of Harm:** Over time, certain toxic behaviors can seem like the norm. Recognizing what is normal versus abnormal becomes blurred, and the person involved may

start justifying or minimizing their partner's behavior.

3. **Impact on Health:** A toxic relationship not only has emotional but also physical manifestations. Stress, insomnia, digestive problems, or even symptoms of post-traumatic disorders can emerge.

4. **External Pressure:** Friends, family, or society can sometimes exert pressure on an individual to maintain a relationship for various reasons, such as cultural expectations or concerns about family "shame." These pressures can make it even more challenging for the individual to recognize or leave a toxic relationship.

5. **Steps Toward Healing:** Once the toxicity of a relationship is recognized, seeking support is crucial. This may include therapy, support groups, or simply talking to trusted individuals. Leaving a harmful relationship is only the first step; healing may take time and resources.

6. **The Importance of Prevention:** Educating oneself about the signs of a toxic relationship and setting clear boundaries from the beginning can help prevent entering harmful relationships in the future.

In conclusion, a relationship should be a source of support, love, and mutual understanding. When these fundamental qualities are lacking or replaced by harmful behaviors, it is essential to have the courage and resources to recognize it and take steps to protect oneself. Every individual has the right to feel valued, respected, and safe in their relationships.

From Dating to a Relationship: The transition from casual dating to a committed and stable relationship is one of the most crucial steps in many people's romantic journey. Every love story is unique, but there are some universal signs and considerations that can guide you in understanding when and how to make this transition effectively and consciously.

1. **Clear Communication:** First and foremost, clarity in communication is essential. If you feel that the relationship is becoming more serious, and you desire a deeper commitment, it's crucial to express your feelings to the other person and see if they reciprocate your emotions and intentions.
2. **Mutual Exclusivity:** Over time, you may start to notice that both of you choose to spend your free time together rather than with other people or potential partners. This is often a sign that both of you see each other as potentially long-term partners.
3. **Shared Values and Life Goals:** Before taking the big step, it's good to assess whether you share similar values and have compatible life

goals. These can include views on family, career, ethical values, and so on.

4. **Meeting Friends and Family:** When you begin introducing your partner to your loved ones and vice versa, it's often a sign that the relationship is becoming more serious, and both of you see a future together.

5. **Discussing Expectations:** Have open discussions about your expectations for the future of the relationship. Do both of you desire a long-term commitment? Are there issues or concerns that need to be addressed?

6. **Facing Challenges Together:** Observe how you handle challenges or conflicts as a couple. If you can navigate through tough times together and find solutions as a team, this is a positive sign for a lasting future relationship.

7. **Timing Assessment:** There's no fixed calendar for when it's the right time to transition from dating to a relationship. For some, it might be after a few weeks, while for others, it might take months. The important thing is that both of you feel ready and are on the same page.

8. **Maintaining Individuality:** Even if you decide to commit to a relationship, it's vital to maintain your individuality. This means respecting personal spaces, having hobbies or personal activities, and not losing sight of who you are as an individual.

9. **Setting Boundaries:** Once you've decided to start a relationship, it's important to establish clear boundaries regarding what both of you are comfortable with, whether related to

communication, intimacy, time expectations, or other areas of your life as a couple.

10.   **Growth and Adaptation:** Remember that relationships require work, understanding, and adaptation. As you transition, it's crucial to remain open to learning and growing with your partner.

Mutual Trust: Trust is the cornerstone of any solid relationship. Building trust takes time, honesty, and consistency. It's not just about being faithful to each other but also being able to rely on each other in times of need, being transparent in your intentions, and demonstrating integrity in every aspect of your life.

Compromise: In any relationship, especially as it becomes more serious, compromise becomes essential. Both partners must be willing to give in on certain points for the sake of the relationship. This doesn't mean sacrificing core values but rather finding common ground on minor issues, like where to spend holidays or how to divide household responsibilities.

Sharing Experiences: Sharing experiences, both positive and negative, can strengthen the bond between two people. Traveling together, facing challenges, celebrating successes, or even spending quiet evenings at home can create lasting memories that form the foundation of your love story.

Financial Commitment: Once the relationship becomes more serious, you may start sharing financial responsibilities, such as rent, bills, or even planning larger purchases like a home or a vacation. Openly discussing finances and establishing a plan on how to manage the financial aspect can prevent future conflicts.

Integration into Each Other's Families: In addition to introducing your partner to your loved ones, a serious relationship may require participation in family events, holidays, and special occasions like weddings or baptisms. These situations can provide an opportunity to better understand each other's backgrounds and values.

Future Planning: While dating may focus on the "here and now," a serious relationship often leads to future planning. This could include discussions about marriage, starting a family, career priorities, and where you want to live in the long term.

Dealing with Challenges: All relationships go through tough periods. Whether it's external stressors like work or health issues or internal tensions like disagreements or misunderstandings, having the skills and patience to address these moments is essential. A strong relationship is built on the ability to overcome adversity together.

Reflection and Self-Analysis: Over time, it's useful for both partners to reflect on the direction the relationship is heading. Are there aspects that could be improved? Are there unresolved issues that need to be addressed? Taking time for introspection can help ensure the relationship remains strong and healthy.

Transitioning from casual dating to a committed relationship is filled with opportunities and challenges. Both partners must be willing to invest, be vulnerable, and learn from each other. With dedication, understanding, and commitment, it is possible to build a solid foundation for a lasting relationship.

In the context of dating and forming lasting relationships, there are additional aspects and reflections to consider:

Clear Expectations: Once a certain level of closeness is reached, it's important for both partners to express their expectations clearly. This may involve matters such as monogamy, involvement with friends and family, or simply how to spend leisure time. Openly communicating your hopes and expectations can prevent potential misunderstandings.

Daily Habits: When you start spending more time together, each person's daily habits and routines become apparent. It might be necessary to make small adjustments in your routines to better integrate each other into your lives. This could include lifestyle choices, sleep patterns, dietary preferences, and more.

Conflict Management: With increased closeness, conflicts may also arise. Instead of avoiding them, it's important to address them maturely, actively listening to each other's perspectives and seeking constructive solutions.

Broadening Horizons: Being in a relationship can also offer the opportunity to explore new activities or interests. Perhaps your partner has hobbies or passions you weren't aware of, and vice versa. Immersing yourselves in new experiences together can strengthen your bond.

Emotional Support: As the relationship deepens, providing mutual emotional support becomes essential. This could mean comforting your partner during times of stress or sadness or celebrating successes together.

Mutual Education: Each individual brings a baggage of experiences, knowledge, and perspectives into the relationship. There is always something new to learn from your partner, whether it's practical skills, cultural insights, or simply a different way of seeing the world.

Health and Well-being: With a more serious relationship, health and well-being topics of each person may emerge, from diet and exercise to mental and emotional health. Supporting each other in these areas can lead to a healthier and happier life together.

Legal and Financial Considerations: At some point, you may start considering more formal aspects of your relationship, such as living together, making joint purchases, or possibly marriage. These decisions can have legal and financial implications that should be carefully considered.

Maintaining Individuality: While it's natural for two people to become closer in a relationship, it's crucial to remember the importance of individuality. Each partner should have space and time for themselves to nurture their interests and maintain a sense of personal identity.

Transitioning from casual dating to a structured relationship is a unique journey for each couple. However, through mutual understanding, communication, and commitment, it's possible to build a solid foundation that can support a lasting and fulfilling relationship.

In conclusion, the transition from casual dating to a stable relationship is a delicate, complex, and often nonlinear process. This crucial phase can determine the stability and resilience of a long-term relationship. Some key factors to keep in mind during this transition include:

Timing and Pace: Not all relationships develop at the same pace. It's essential to respect your own and your partner's timing. Pushing too hard or too fast can cause tensions, while proceeding too slowly might indicate a lack of interest or commitment.

Communication: During this phase, keeping channels of communication open and honest is fundamental. Discussing feelings, expectations, and concerns can help both partners better understand the direction the relationship is heading and address any issues before they become insurmountable.

Awareness: As you approach a deeper commitment, it's crucial to reflect on what you truly desire in a relationship and whether your current partner fulfills those desires. You should never transition into a serious relationship just for the sake of it or due to external pressures.

Assessment of Values and Goals: Sharing core values and life goals can be a strong indicator of long-term compatibility. If there are fundamental divergences, it's time to address them and consider whether they can be resolved.

Intimacy and Vulnerability: As the relationship deepens, you expose yourself more significantly to your partner. This vulnerability can be daunting but is also a crucial part of building a deep and meaningful connection.

Practical Considerations: At some point, discussions about practical matters such as cohabitation, shared finances, or future planning may arise. These discussions can reveal further compatibility or areas of concern.

External Support: Friends, family, and counselors can offer valuable external perspectives on the relationship. While the final decision always rests with the couple, taking external feedback into consideration can be helpful.

In summary, transitioning from dating to a serious relationship requires reflection, communication, and commitment from both parties. Every relationship is unique, but approaching this phase with openness, honesty, and care can help couples build a solid foundation for a lasting bond.

18. The Role of Intimacy: • Addressing Physical and Emotional Intimacy in a Relationship.

Intimacy, both physical and emotional, is a fundamental component of romantic relationships. It represents the depth of connection between two individuals, influencing the quality and duration of the relationship itself. Let's delve into the various aspects and facets of intimacy in relationships:

Emotional Intimacy: Emotional intimacy is the ability to share one's feelings, fears, hopes, and dreams with a partner, feeling understood and accepted. It concerns the depth of emotional connection between two people, the level of mutual trust, and the ability to be vulnerable with each other.

1. **Vulnerability:** To achieve genuine emotional intimacy, it's essential to allow oneself to be vulnerable. This means opening up sincerely, expressing one's feelings, even those of insecurity or fear.
2. **Active Listening:** Intimacy grows when you sincerely listen to your partner, seeking to understand their feelings and concerns without judgment.
3. **Empathy:** Feeling with your partner, not just for them, is a key element of emotional intimacy. Empathy allows for a deeper connection by showing understanding and support.

Physical Intimacy: Physical intimacy refers to the physical connection and contact between two people. It can range from affectionate gestures, such as holding hands or hugging, to moments of heightened passion and sexual intimacy.

1. **Expression of Desire:** The ability to openly communicate one's physical desires and needs is essential for building satisfying physical intimacy.
2. **Body Awareness:** Being comfortable with one's body and understanding its needs is

fundamental to building a genuine physical connection with a partner.

3. **Respecting Boundaries:** Each individual has different boundaries when it comes to physical intimacy. Respecting and clearly communicating them is essential for building trust and understanding.

Balancing Emotional and Physical Intimacy: Emotional and physical intimacy do not always progress at the same pace in a relationship. A couple may have deep emotional intimacy but struggle to find a physical connection, and vice versa.

1. **Communication:** Openly discussing your needs and expectations helps find a balance between physical and emotional intimacy.
2. **Patience:** There may be times when one type of intimacy lags behind. Being patient and giving your partner time to open up or adjust is crucial.

Challenges and Obstacles: Some people may find it difficult to address intimacy due to past traumas, personal insecurities, or previous toxic relationships. It's essential to recognize these obstacles and, if necessary, seek external or therapeutic support to address them.

In summary, intimacy, both emotional and physical, is an essential aspect of relationships. It requires communication, understanding, respect, and commitment from both parties to fully develop and support an authentic and lasting connection.

Intimacy in a relationship is not a static concept but evolves and changes over time, based on life stages, experiences, and personal changes for each partner. It's an intricate dance of emotions, sensations, and desires that must be continually balanced and renegotiated.

Let's further explore this concept by delving into the different dimensions of intimacy:

Mental Connection: In addition to emotional and physical intimacy, there is intellectual intimacy. This type of connection develops when two people share thoughts, ideas, and deep discussions. A stimulating conversation can be as intimate and fulfilling as a hug or a kiss.

Spiritual Intimacy: Some couples find a deep connection through spirituality or religion. This type of intimacy can manifest in various forms, such as shared prayer, meditation, or participation in religious rituals together. Spiritual intimacy can provide a solid foundation of shared values and beliefs.

Intimacy Through Shared Interests: Sharing hobbies and passions can strengthen the bond between two people. Whether it's cooking together, hiking, or watching movies, these shared activities can become special moments of connection.

Routine and Daily Intimacy: Intimacy doesn't always manifest in grand gestures or deep discussions. Sometimes, it's found in small things, like having breakfast together every morning, exchanging messages during the day, or simply falling asleep next to each other every night.

Challenges to Intimacy: Various factors can hinder intimacy in a relationship. Stress, health issues, work problems, or family issues can create barriers. In these moments, it's essential to recognize the importance of seeking moments of connection, even if they are brief or simple.

Technology and Intimacy: We live in an era where technology plays a predominant role in our daily lives. While it can help maintain a connection with your partner, especially when apart, it can also become a barrier if used excessively. Finding a balance and ensuring that you dedicate time to face-to-face connection is crucial.

The Need for Space: While intimacy is fundamental, recognizing the value of personal space is equally important. Each individual needs time for themselves to reflect, recharge, or simply relax.

Overall, intimacy in a relationship is a mosaic of different connections intertwining. It's a journey of discovery and mutual understanding that requires commitment, communication, and love. Every relationship has its unique rhythm, and finding the right balance of intimacy is a process that develops and changes over time.

Relationships Beyond Traditional Definitions: Exploring the Complexity of Intimacy

Beyond traditional definitions, intimacy extends far beyond the physical or emotional sphere, becoming a profound understanding and interconnection between individuals. Various facets of intimacy can further illuminate its complexity and depth:

Intimacy as Empathic Resonance: When two people are intimately connected, they often can "feel" each other's emotions, even without words. This empathic resonance allows each partner to perceive joy, pain, excitement, or sadness in the other, creating a deep bond that goes beyond mere understanding.

Growth Through Vulnerability: Showing vulnerability is a crucial aspect of intimacy. It reveals who we truly are, with all our strengths and flaws. Through vulnerability, we display our true essence to our partner, allowing for an authentic connection.

Intimacy as Reflection: In a deeply intimate relationship, the partner often serves as a mirror, reflecting aspects of ourselves that we may not see. This can lead to profound personal realizations and mutual growth.

Intimacy and History: Over time, the shared history between partners becomes a form of intimacy in itself. Shared memories, challenges overcome together, and adventures experienced contribute to forming a unique bond that only those two people can fully understand.

The Art of Non-Communication: Sometimes, intimacy doesn't require words. It can be found in shared silence, a gaze, or a simple gesture. These moments of non-communication can often convey more than a thousand words.

Intimacy in Difficult Times: It's easy to feel connected when everything is going well, but true intimacy also reveals itself in times of crisis. How a couple faces challenges together, supports each other, and navigates storms can reveal the depth of their connection.

Adaptation and Change: People change over time, and so do relationships. Intimacy requires ongoing adaptability, recognizing and embracing changes in oneself and one's partner.

Boundaries and Intimacy: While intimacy implies closeness and connection, it's also essential to recognize and respect boundaries. Each individual has personal limits, and a part of intimacy is learning where these boundaries are and how to respect them.

Intimacy Beyond the Couple: Although we primarily discuss intimacy in a romantic context, it's essential to recognize that intimacy can exist in many other forms. Deep friendships, family bonds, and even connections with pets can offer levels of intimacy that enrich our human experience.

In summary, intimacy is a multifaceted concept, an ever-evolving journey that requires attention, care, and profound self-awareness and awareness of the other. Through intimacy, we are invited to see and be seen, to know and be known in ways that deeply enrich our experience of life and relationships.

Understanding Intimacy in a Relationship Beyond the Physical Presence

Understanding intimacy in a relationship goes far beyond mere physical presence or familiarity with one's partner. Intimacy, in its purest essence, is the fusion of souls, minds, and bodies in a union that transcends mere physical presence. It is the ability to see and be seen, to understand and be understood, without judgment and with complete acceptance.

Emotional Depth: Intimacy is rooted in the depths of shared emotions. It allows each partner to feel safe, welcomed, and loved for who they truly are, without masks or defenses. This emotional depth can offer a sense of belonging and connection that is rare and precious.

Vulnerability: At the heart of intimacy lies vulnerability. It involves breaking down barriers, exposing our insecurities, fears, hopes, and dreams to our partner. This openness allows for a level of understanding and connection that wouldn't otherwise be possible.

Empathic Resonance: Intimacy also manifests through deep mutual empathy, where each individual can perceive and resonate with the other's emotions. This creates a cycle of understanding and support, further strengthening the bond between partners.

Growth and Adaptation: True intimacy is not static. It evolves and grows over time, adapting to the challenges and changes that each partner experiences in life. This ability to grow together, rather than separately, is essential for maintaining a deep and meaningful connection.

Respecting Boundaries: While seeking deep intimacy, it's crucial to recognize and respect personal boundaries. This balance between closeness and individual space allows for a healthy and mutually respectful connection.

In conclusion, intimacy is one of the fundamental pillars of a healthy and fulfilling relationship. It must be nurtured with care, attention, and commitment from both partners. When authentic and mutual, intimacy can elevate a relationship above the daily challenges, creating a bond that can withstand life's storms. Through intimacy, people not only share their physical existence but merge on emotional, mental, and spiritual levels, experiencing the beauty and depth of an authentic and lasting connection.

19. Conflict Management: Techniques and Advice for Addressing and Resolving Conflicts in a Relationship

Conflict management is a crucial element in every relationship. All relationships, no matter how strong or healthy, inevitably face moments of disagreement or tension. However, the ability to handle these moments with maturity and understanding can make the difference between a relationship that strengthens through challenges and one that weakens and potentially breaks apart.

Active Listening: Before responding or reacting to a conflict, it's essential to listen carefully to what the other person has to say. This doesn't just mean hearing the words but also trying to understand the emotions and feelings behind those words. Active listening requires a conscious effort to put oneself in the other person's shoes and see the situation from their perspective.

Nonviolent Communication: This technique focuses on expressing one's feelings and needs honestly but non-accusatorily. It involves speaking in the first person, avoiding blaming or criticizing the partner. For example, instead of saying, "You make me feel ignored," one could say, "I feel ignored when you don't pay attention."

Taking Breaks: If a discussion is becoming particularly heated or emotional, taking a break can be helpful. This gives both partners the opportunity to cool off, reflect, and return to the issue with a clearer mind.

Mutual Respect: Even in times of disagreement, it's crucial to maintain a sense of mutual respect. This means avoiding shouting, insulting, or making derogatory comments. Respect is the foundation on which trust and understanding are built.

Seeking Compromise Solutions: Often, conflicts arise from differences in opinion or desires. Instead of trying to "win" the argument, it's helpful to seek solutions that can satisfy both parties, even if it means making concessions.

Professional Consultation: If conflicts become frequent or particularly severe, seeking the help of a couples therapist or mediator may be useful. These professionals can provide tools and techniques to help couples communicate more effectively and resolve conflicts.

While conflict management is a complex art, it can be further explored from many angles, analyzing additional nuances and details related to it. The ability to manage conflicts is not only a key skill for maintaining healthy relationships but can also impact personal growth and emotional well-being.

Self-Awareness: Understanding oneself and one's emotional reactions is the first step in effectively managing conflicts. Asking why a particular situation or comment triggers a specific reaction can help identify personal insecurities or sensitive points. Once identified, it becomes easier to address and communicate them to the partner.

Avoiding Absolute Language: Using words like "always" or "never" can generalize and worsen a conflict. For example, saying, "You never listen to me" can sound like an absolute accusation, while "Sometimes, I feel unheard" leaves room for dialogue and understanding.

Constructive Feedback: Instead of focusing solely on what's wrong, it's helpful to present things in a positive light, suggesting how they could improve. This approach is less likely to put the partner on the defensive and paves the way for more productive communication.

Empathy: Try to imagine how you would feel if you were in your partner's shoes. This perspective can help understand their actions and reactions, even if you don't agree with them. Empathy can create a more compassionate environment for resolving disagreements.

Avoiding Stagnation: When a conflict seems to go in circles without a solution in sight, it can be useful to change the approach or environment. Sometimes, taking a walk or moving the conversation to a different place can help break the deadlock.

Accepting Differences: Not all issues will be resolved with mutual agreement. Sometimes, accepting that you have different opinions and agreeing to disagree may be the best way to move forward.

Remembering the Big Picture: Amid a conflict, it can be easy to lose sight of the bigger picture. However, it's essential to remember why you are in that relationship and what positive aspects make it special. This can help put things into perspective and focus on what truly matters.

Establishing "Rules": Some couples find it helpful to establish basic conflict rules, such as not going to bed angry or never raising one's voice. These rules can serve as guidelines to ensure that disagreements remain productive and respectful.

Furthermore, in the context of conflict management in a relationship, it's important to remember that every person and every couple is unique. What works for one couple may not work for another. The key is to find a balance and techniques that fit one's specific needs and dynamics.

Nonverbal Communication: Besides words, our bodies communicate a lot. Eyes, posture, and tone of voice can convey powerful messages. For instance, a cold tone of voice or an evasive gaze can communicate distance or anger, even if the spoken words are neutral. Being aware of your own nonverbal communication and correctly interpreting your partner's can make a significant difference in mutual understanding.

Respect for Timing: If one partner is not ready to discuss or is too emotional, it can be beneficial to postpone the conversation to a later time when both can talk with a cooler head.

Couples Therapy: In some cases, seeking the help of a professional, such as a couples therapist, can be useful. These specialists are trained to assist couples in navigating conflicts, offering tools and strategies to improve communication and mutual understanding.

Acknowledging Your Own Mistakes: Humility plays a crucial role in conflict management. Recognizing when you've been wrong or could have handled a situation better is essential for building trust and intimacy.

Active Listening: This technique involves listening carefully to what the other person is saying without interrupting and then paraphrasing or repeating what has been said to ensure you've understood correctly. Active listening can prevent misunderstandings and show your partner that you genuinely care about what they have to say.

Stress Management: External stressors, like work or financial concerns, can influence the relationship dynamic. Finding ways to manage individual stress, such as meditation, physical exercise, or spending time in nature, can prevent unnecessary conflicts caused by external tensions.

Self-Education: Numerous books, courses, and seminars focus on the art of communication and conflict management in relationships. Investing time in self-education in these areas can offer new perspectives and useful tools.

Conflict as an Opportunity: Instead of viewing conflict as a problem, it can be seen as an opportunity to grow and deepen the connection in the relationship. By addressing issues head-on and overcoming challenges together, couples can strengthen their bond and build a stronger foundation for the future.

Overall, it's essential to remember that conflicts are a natural part of every relationship. What truly matters is how they are handled and how they can be used as a springboard for deeper connection and stronger love.

Understanding Conflict in Relationships: An In-Depth Reflection

Conflict Origins: At the core of every conflict, there is often a difference in opinions, values, expectations, or needs. These differences can stem from diverse cultural, educational, or family backgrounds, past relationship experiences, or life dynamics, such as work-related stress or the arrival of a child.

The Importance of Communication: The key to resolving conflicts lies in the ability to communicate effectively. This doesn't just mean talking; it means sharing feelings, needs, and concerns in a way that the other partner can understand. The goal is not to win an argument but to find a joint solution that satisfies both parties.

Empathy: Putting oneself in the other's shoes is fundamental. Empathy allows seeing the situation from another perspective and understanding the other's reasons and emotions. Such understanding can often reduce tensions and facilitate a solution.

Managing Emotions: During a conflict, emotions can become intense. Recognizing and managing one's own emotions are crucial to avoid escalation. This may include taking a break, deep breathing, or even postponing the discussion if necessary.

Boundaries and Limits: In every relationship, it's important to establish and respect certain boundaries. This includes acceptable behavior during a dispute. For example, yelling, insulting, or using offensive language should be avoided.

Building Solutions: Instead of focusing solely on the problem, couples should work together to find solutions. This may require compromises from both sides, but ultimately, it can lead to a solution that strengthens the relationship.

Prevention: Once common causes of conflict are identified, couples can work to prevent them in the future. This might involve scheduling regular check-ins, establishing new routines, or adopting stress management techniques.

Experts and Therapy: If conflicts persist and adopted strategies don't seem to work, consulting a couples therapist or another professional may be helpful. Sometimes, having a neutral third party can help identify deep-seated issues and work on solutions.

In conclusion, addressing conflicts in a relationship is not only inevitable but can also be constructive. If handled correctly, conflicts can offer opportunities for growth, deeper mutual understanding, and strengthening the bond between partners. The essence lies in the approach: addressing conflicts with love, respect, and the goal of mutual understanding can transform these moments into significant milestones in a couple's history.

Conclusion: Reflections on the Art of Dating

Throughout this extensive journey through the various aspects of the dating world, we've explored diverse themes, from the practical details of online dating to chemistry, managing rejection and conflicts, to personal growth and intimacy management. These reflections aim to construct a holistic view of what it means to venture into the vast world of dating in such a complex and ever-evolving era.

But beyond techniques, tips, and strategies, there's a central message that emerges: the importance of authenticity and self-confidence.

Authenticity: It's easy to get lost in the whirlwind of dating, trying to fit into what we think might please someone else or what society tells us we should be. However, true connection is built on being true to oneself and to others. This doesn't mean there aren't moments of adaptation or compromise, but at the core of one's essence, a woman should feel free to be herself.

Confidence: Confidence isn't just about feeling secure in relation to your partner or the dating environment, but also about believing in oneself, one's worth, and one's ability to make decisions. Every woman has the right to feel valued, respected, and loved for who she truly is.

Challenges and Growth: Every stage of life presents its challenges, and the dating world is no exception. But as with any challenge, there is always an opportunity for growth. Every date, every relationship, whether it lasts for one night or a lifetime, offers valuable lessons that can enrich the soul and deepen self-understanding.

Looking Forward: Women today are challenging and redefining traditional gender roles and societal expectations in many areas of life, including dating. And while there might be external pressure to conform to certain standards or models, it's essential to remember that every person has their unique love journey and path of discovery.

Ultimately, the key to successfully navigating the dating world is to do so with authenticity, self-compassion, and openness to the infinite possibilities life has to offer. So, to all the women embarking on this journey, I encourage you to do it with confidence and courage, knowing that every step, every experience, will contribute to shaping the unique and precious tapestry of your love story.

Book Conclusion: The Odyssey of Dating - A Journey of Growth and Authenticity

The art of dating is not only a journey to find a partner but also a journey of self-discovery. Throughout this book, we have navigated through twenty essential chapters that provide a comprehensive overview of what it means to venture into the world of dating in the 21st century.

Useful Resources: If you wish to delve deeper or seek support in your dating journey, here are some online resources and guides that may be helpful:

1. **OkCupid Blog:** A blog offering data-driven insights into dating.

2. **Dr. Alexandra Solomon:** A psychologist providing advice on relationships and love.

3. **Relate Institute:** A space providing resources and tools for healthy relationships.

4. **PsychCentral:** Articles and advice on emotional well-being and relationships.

Additionally, there are many guides and books that delve into specific topics covered in our book. Be sure to do your research and find what resonates with you and your personal situation.

In conclusion, dating is a journey, not a destination. As you navigate this path, remember to remain authentic, open, and confident, knowing that every experience contributes to your ongoing journey of growth and self-discovery.

Good luck!

Milton Keynes UK
Ingram Content Group UK Ltd.
UKHW020238221123
432980UK00016B/1166